The Institute of Chartered Financial Analysts
Continuing Education Series

Innovations in Fixed-Income Instruments and Markets

Washington, D.C.
March 24, 1987

Michael R. Asay

Delores S. Driscoll, CFA

Anthony V. Dub

Jay W. Forrester

James Grant

Rodney L. Gray

Michael S. Ivanovitch

Joel W. Miller

Frederic A. Nelson III

William H. Pike, CFA

Paul A. Volcker

Brian F. Wruble, CFA

Michael L. Youngblood

Edited by
Richard W. McEnally, CFA

Katrina F. Sherrerd, *Managing Editor*
Susan S. Brennan, *Associate Editor*

Sponsored by
The Institute of Chartered
Financial Analysts

Additional copies of this publication may be ordered from

Professional Book Distributors, Inc.
P.O. Box 100120
Roswell, GA 30077
1–800-848–0773

This publication is designed to provide accurate
and authoritative information in regard to the subject matter
covered. It is sold with the understanding that the
publisher is not engaged in rendering legal, accounting, or
other professional service. If legal advice or other
expert assistance is required, the services of a competent
professional should be sought.

*From a Declaration of Principles jointly adopted by a Committee
of the American Bar Association and a Committee of Publishers.*

ISBN 0–935015-04–3

Printed in the United States of America

Table of Contents

Foreword

Innovations in the fixed-income markets have increased at a staggering pace. With the advent of these innovative new instruments, fixed-income management has changed dramatically at most institutions.

A number of the new fixed-income instruments and their impact on institutional fixed-income management were examined at the seminar "Innovations in Fixed-Income Instruments and Markets," sponsored by the Institute of Chartered Financial Analysts on March 24, 1987 in Washington, D.C. This publication is the result of that seminar.

The Institute wishes to acknowledge Robert C. Beck and John Beck of Beck, Mack & Oliver, and Edwin H. Yeo of the Yeo Farms for their efforts in arranging the participation of Federal Reserve Chairman Paul A. Volcker in this seminar.

We also wish to extend our appreciation to the seminar moderator, Delores S. Driscoll, CFA, Standish Ayer & Wood, Inc.; and to the seminar speakers: Michael R. Asay, Vice President, Goldman Sachs and Company; Anthony V. Dub, Managing Director, The First Boston Corporation; Jay W. Forrester, Germeshausen Professor of Management, Alfred P. Sloan School of Management, Massachusetts Institute of Technology; James Grant, Publisher, Grant's *Interest Rate Observer*; Rodney L. Gray, Treasurer, Transco Energy Company; Michael S. Ivanovitch, International Investment Advisor; Joel W. Miller, Vice President, Lazard Freres & Co.; Frederic A. Nelson, Manager of Passive Investments, Bankers Trust Company; William H. Pike, CFA, Vice President, High Income Fund, Fidelity Management and Research Company; Paul A. Volcker, Chairman, Board of Governors of the Federal Reserve System; Brian F. Wruble, CFA, President and Chief Executive Officer, Equitable Capital Management Corp.; Michael D. Youngblood, Vice President and Manager, Residential Mortgage Research, Salomon Brothers Inc.

Special thanks are extended to Richard W. McEnally, CFA for his valuable contribution as editor of this publication, and to Darwin M. Bayston, CFA, and Susan D. Martin, CFA, for their roles in the organization of the conference.

Katrina F. Sherrerd
Assistant Vice President
Education and Research

Biographies of Speakers

Michael R. Asay, Ph.D. is Vice President of Mortgage Securities Research at Goldman, Sachs and Company, where his responsibilities include new product development, structured transactions, and asset/liability management. Dr. Asay is also responsible for the development and management of the analytics of CMO residuals, stripped mortgage-backed securities and their use in portfolio restructuring, and interest rate and prepayment risk management. Previously, he was head of mortgage research at Citibank Investment Bank, and head of new product development and marketing financial futures at the Chicago Mercantile Exchange. Dr. Asay holds a Ph.D. from the University of Southern California.

Dolores Stang Driscoll, CFA, is Vice President and Director of Bond Research at Standish, Ayer & Wood, Inc., and is Chairman of their Pension Committee. Ms. Driscoll is responsible for institutional bond portfolio management and also directs research on mortgages, original issue discount bonds, innovative securities, and financial futures. Ms. Driscoll is a Chartered Investment Counsellor and a member of the Boston Security Analysts Society, and serves as Director of the Bond Analysts Society of Boston, which she co-founded in 1976. Ms. Driscoll holds an A.B. from Indiana University and an M.B.A. from Boston University.

Anthony V. Dub is Managing Director in the Corporate Finance Department of The First Boston Corporation. Mr. Dub is head of First Boston's Asset Finance Group, which develops non-mortgage, asset-related financing. In addition, he is responsible for a number of the firm's major accounts, and serves as a member of its Investment Banking Committee. Previously, he headed First Boston's Markets Group, and has also worked with the firm's International Finance Group. Mr. Dub is a graduate of Princeton University.

Jay W. Forrester is Germeshausen Professor of Management at the Massachusetts Institute of Technology (MIT), where he directs the System Dynamics Program in the Alfred P. Sloan School of Management. Professor Forrester, whose career with MIT spans four decades, is a pioneer in the field of system dynamics, which involves the use of computer models to evaluate the effects of alternative policies on growth, stability, fluctuation, and changing behavior in corporations, cities, and countries. Prior to joining the Sloan School, Professor Forrester served as Director of the MIT Digital Computer Laboratory, and was head of the Digital Computer Division of MIT's Lincoln Laboratory. He is the author of several books on system dynamics and has received numerous national and international awards. Professor Forrester was inducted into the National Inventors Hall of Fame in 1979. He holds a B.S. from the University of Nebraska and an S.M. from MIT, as well as honorary degrees from a number of universities, including the University of Notre Dame University and the University of Mannheim.

James Grant is Publisher of *Grant's Interest Rate Observer*, a bimonthly publication devoted to the credit markets. Previously, Mr. Grant was on the staff of Barron's, where he originated the credit-markets column, "Current Yield." He is the author of *Bernard M. Baruch: The Adventures of a Wall Street Legend*, and has written for publications as diverse as *American Spectator* and *The New Republic*. Mr. Grant holds a bachelor's degree from Indiana University and a master's degree from Columbia University.

Rodney L. Gray is Treasurer of Transco Energy Company, responsible for corporate Treasury and Investment Services. Prior to becoming Treasurer, Mr. Gray was Manager of the Treasury and Assistant Treasurer at Transco. He is a Certified Public Accountant and a member of the Texas Society of Certified Public Accountants, the American Institute of Certified Public Accountants, and the National Association of

Corporate Treasurers. Mr. Gray holds a B.S. from Rocky Mountain College and a B.S. from the University of Wyoming.

Michael S. Ivanovitch, Ph.D. is an investment advisor based in Paris. Dr. Ivanovitch has published numerous articles on international economics and finance, and lectures frequently to groups of economists, bankers, institutional investors, and business professionals. He teaches economics at Columbia University and at H.E.C., a leading European business school located in Paris. Dr. Ivanovitch holds an M.A., an M.B.A., and a Ph.D. from Columbia University, as well as a European law degree.

Joel W. Miller is a Fixed Income Tactician at Lazard Freres & Company, and directs the firm's bond dedication and immunization efforts. Mr. Miller's previous experience includes the development of a debt retirement model at Morgan Stanley, which resulted in the first zero coupon versus full coupon debt exchanges. He also developed the Stuart Brothers Sinking Fund book. Mr. Miller holds a B.S. from Columbia University.

Frederic A. "Rick" Nelson III is Vice President and Manager of Passive Investments at Bankers Trust Company. His group is responsible for investing assets, employing vehicles such as domestic and international equity index funds, bond index funds, and stock index futures. Mr. Nelson holds a B.S. from the Wharton School, University of Pennsylvania and an M.B.A. from the University of Chicago.

William H. Pike, CFA, is a Vice President and Portfolio Manager with Fidelity Management and Research Company, where he is responsible for the firm's High Income Fund and high-income institutional accounts. Mr. Pike has also worked as an Industry Specialist and Securities Analyst during his career with the firm. Prior to his association with Fidelity Management, he was a Securities Analyst with Old Colony Trust Company and The Boston Company. Mr. Pike holds a B.S. from the Massachusetts Institute of Technology and an M.B.A. from Columbia University.

Paul A. Volcker is currently serving his second four-year term as Chairman of the Board of Governors of the Federal Reserve System, and is also Chairman of the Federal Open Market Committee. Previously, Mr. Volcker was President of the Federal Reserve Bank of New York, and also served as Under Secretary of the Treasury. He has held office at the Treasury and within the Federal Reserve System under Presidents Johnson, Nixon, Carter, and Reagan. During his tenure at the Treasury, Mr. Volcker was instrumental in revising the international monetary system; he also was a member of the board of the Overseas Private Investment Corporation and of the Federal National Mortgage Association. He received the Alexander Hamilton Award in recognition of his service at the Treasury. Mr. Volcker holds a B.A. from Princeton University and an M.A. from Harvard University, and has received honorary degrees from such institutions as Notre Dame University, Columbia University, Johns Hopkins University, and Yale University.

Brian F. Wruble, CFA, is Chairman, President, and Chief Executive Officer of Equitable Capital Management Corp., a wholly-owned subsidiary of Equitable Life, where he is also Executive Vice President and a member of the Investment Policy Committee. Previously, Mr. Wruble spent 10 years on Wall Street, most recently with Smith Barney, Harris Upham and Co., where he was Co-Manager of Fundamental Equities Research. Mr. Wruble serves as a Director of Advanced Systems Applications, Inc., and Chairman and President of Equitable Realty Asset Corporation. He also serves on the Editorial Review Board of *The CFA Digest*. Mr. Wruble holds Bachelor's and Master's degrees from Cornell University and an M.B.A. from New York University.

Michael D. Youngblood, Ph.D. is Vice President and Manager, Residential Mortgage Research at Salomon Brothers Inc, where his responsibilities include analysis of mortgage securities as well as new product development. Previous experience includes extensive analysis of mortgage security products at savings & loan institutions, including the development of various modeling techniques. He has lectured at both the University of London and the University of Texas. Dr. Youngblood holds a B.A. from the University of Texas at Austin, an M.A. from the University of Pennsylvania, and a Ph.D. from Bedford College, University of London.

Overview of the Seminar

Richard W. McEnally, CFA

The proceedings of this seminar deal with a variety of innovations in fixed-income instruments, markets, and management that have occurred in the past six or so years. These include: 1) extensive public issuance of securities that are below investment grade at the time of issue—so-called junk bonds; 2) the unbundling and repackaging of existing securities in ways that increase their attractiveness to investors, as typified by the new securities that have been created from single-family mortgages; 3) the creation of securities that combine debt features and options on commodities—or asset-linked debt securities; 4) the indexation of fixed-income securities portfolios, paralleling a development that began in equity portfolios well over a decade ago; 5) securitization, or the conversion of financial assets that previously had no public market into traded securities; and 6) globalization, or international fixed-income investment, which also parallels a development that began in equity portfolios over a decade ago.

A number of the speakers discuss reasons for this upsurge of innovation in fixed-income securities and markets, so no effort will be made to explore the question of "Why?" in this introduction. A few miscellaneous observations, however, may be useful in putting these innovations into perspective.

Fixed-income securities, like other securities, are really nothing more than traded contracts. As contracts, they are created with the pen rather than the lathe—that is, there are no physical constraints on what can be created; the only real constraint is that they pass legal standards. Therefore, the potential for creative securities innovation is virtually endless. The challenge is to devise securities that add value to the system by allowing participants to finance and invest in ways that were unavailable previously, or to allow them to do so more efficiently than was previously possible.

The risks that ultimately matter in the economy are the risks that cannot be eliminated by financial arrangements, such as the danger of economic downturn. Securities innovation can do nothing about these fundamental risks. Financial markets can provide a real service to the economy, however, by eliminating nonfundamental risks, or risks that do not need to be taken. For example, long-duration bonds represent clear risks to market participants with short investment horizons, while short-duration bonds present risks to long-horizon market participants. The obvious solution to dealing with these risks—the solution that financial markets should provide—is to finesse them by making it easy for the long-horizon investors to hold the long-duration securities, and visa versa. The increased potential for the reallocation and neutralization of risks permitted by securities innovation promises to make a real contribution to our economy and society.

The repackaging of risks is not without its dangers, however. When certain types of risk are concentrated in specific securities forms, rather than being spread out over a variety of securities, there is increased potential for the unwary to be badly hurt, as several major investment banks recently discovered the hard way.

Financial markets also create value by providing access and liquidity. Basic attitudes towards junk bonds, for example, may vary widely. The fact is, however, that both investors and borrowers are better off if investors who would like to own junk bonds, but were previously unable to obtain them due to the lack of a meaningful public market, may now do so.

Many of the innovations of our day are nothing more than the outcome of the application of plain common sense. For example, non-dollar bond markets account for about half the value of the world's fixed-income securities, and it is obvious that international interest rates and currencies behave in anything but uniform fashion. Therefore, provided the frictions are not too great, the logic of globalization is virtually inescapable. A common-sense case may also be made for indexation.

One of the most valuable innovations is the

unbundling of the typical fixed-income security. The point is illustrated with the following example. Suppose you go to the grocery store, and as you walk across the parking lot a man comes up to you with a bag of groceries. He shows you his receipt and offers to sell you the bag of groceries for just what he paid for it. The chances are that you would not accept this offer despite the time you would save, because his tastes are not your tastes. For many years, issuers offered everyone essentially the same grocery bag of bond characteristics, even though the contents of the bag suited the tastes of only a few investors. With unbundling, investors may go into the grocery store and pull the bond features off the shelf to make up a grocery bag that suits their own tastes. They must be better off as a result.

One implication of unbundling is that innovative securities that are complex combinations of existing securities may not have much appeal in the marketplace. Therefore, for example, it is highly unlikely that specific forms of asset-linked securities are going to be very successful because they are not going to be equally attractive to all investors and issuers. The needs of the marketplace are probably much better served by the separate offering of a debt security and a long-term option on the asset in question, enabling investors or issuers to mix and match as they see fit.

Finally, the history of innovation in most fields is that only a very few are successful and survive for any meaningful period of time; most innovations fall by the wayside, presumably because they do not meet real needs or simply do not work well. These principles should also apply to securities innovation, especially when "working well" includes being reasonably easy to understand and analyze. A number of recent securities innovations border on being little more than gimmicks, devised by hungry investment bankers in the hope that they will catch on in the marketplace. Some of these securities may come to present real opportunities for investors who take the trouble to understand them and who have needs that map closely with the securities' characteristics. There is a danger, however, that many investors will be left with "orphan" securities that do not suit their needs and have essentially no secondary market.

OPENING REMARKS

Delores Driscoll provides an introduction to the conference. Driscoll underscores the explosion of innovations that has occurred in the fixed-income securities area in recent years, and briefly reviews some factors that have brought about this explosion. These include:

- Deregulation of the banking and financial system, which has led to new emphasis on the liability management of financial institutions and a desire to securitize the assets of these institutions;
- The restructuring of corporate America, and with it the emergence and rapid growth of debt securities that do not meet traditional standards of quality;
- Exchange-rate volatility and a heightened awareness of the importance of world financial markets, encouraging the globalization of fixed-income investment;
- Increased competition among both securities dealers and investment managers, promoting the creation of new securities forms by the dealers, and leading to boldness and innovation in seeking enhanced returns and better risk control by the investment managers.

Driscoll concludes by observing that this innovation has bred a climate of excitement, and has expanded opportunities to both make money and lose it. On a more contrarian note, she cautions that not all innovations are good; when carefully analyzed, some have spurious benefits and high costs.

INNOVATIONS IN PERSPECTIVE

Brian Wruble takes a broad view of financial innovations and concludes that they are intertwined with the essence of financial transactions. Transactions take place only when the transacting parties have different viewpoints or different needs; the transactions occur because they increase the utility of the parties. Financial innovations increase the utility-creating potential of the transacting process because they allow the participants to concentrate on those activities in which they have a comparative advantage. The example he reviews is that of the savings and loan industry. Savings and loan institutions have a comparative advantage in mortgage loan origination, but because of their short-term liability structure they are not well positioned to bear the interest-rate risk associated with traditional fixed-rate mortgages. Two innovations have come to their rescue. Securitization allows savings and loans to pass mortgages along to investors who are better able to hold them because these investors have long liabilities; and adjustable-rate mortgages allow savings and loans to pass the interest-rate risk to the borrowers.

Wruble feels that the pace of financial innovation has increased for three reasons: (1) increased volatility of interest rates, which is magnified by the high leverage of many financial institutions; (2) a greater understanding on the part of the institutions of their comparative advantages; and (3) a critical mass in the resources needed to deal with innovations, ranging from communications methodology to numerical processing capability to analytical models.

Wruble sees these three considerations coming together to create innovation that leads to greatly increased efficiency in financial markets. The process is facilitated by the wealth creation and redistribution that results from the innovation, leading, according to Wruble, to the "best and the brightest" being attracted to contribute to the innovative process.

He concludes his observations with a brief analysis of categories of fixed-income innovation, which include:

- Cash-market innovations, consisting of new fundamental securities such as stripped instruments, asset-backed securities, and high-yield bonds;
- Derivative securities and arrangements, such as futures on financial instruments and interest-rate swaps;
- Management strategies, such as hedging, dynamic asset allocation, and immunization;
- New analytics, such as duration, convexity, and the ability to value the option features in many fixed-income securities.

THE HIGH-YIELD BOND MARKET

This session presents conflicting views of the high-yield bond market. The first speaker, James Grant, is unabashedly negative. He begins by observing that credit is sick; this observation is based on the record number of bond defaults and downgrades in the past year. Yet all these developments appear to be largely ignored by the participants in the credit markets.

He next observes that the junk bond market is not large in the scheme of things, but it is interesting and worthy of study at least in part because it is symptomatic of the times and because it illustrates what he calls the credit cycle. This is the evolution of attitudes toward low-quality credits that initially involves skepticism, high risk premia, and high returns; gradually shifts towards acceptance of decreasing credit quality, lower risk premia, and low returns; and culminates in a phase of manic optimism that ends with high defaults and great losses. According to Grant, there is a precedent for this cycle in the history of foreign sovereign bond issuance in the United States in the 1920s and 1930s.

Grant indicates that one cannot be sure when the manic phase has been reached and risk begins to eclipse reward, but that point must be close. He believes that in the present environment, investment bankers are reaching for fees and investment mangers are reaching for yield. Attitudes of credulity, faith, conviction, and optimism have replaced the skepticism and aversion to risk that characterize the periods in which investment in low-quality credits is rewarding.

William Pike takes a more sanguine view of the high-yield bond market. He acknowledges that it is controversial, but suggests that this reflects the newness of the area, the lack of knowledge and understanding about it, and the fixed-income mentality that is traditionally highly risk averse. Pike extends Grant's analogy: If credit is sick and high-income bonds are the terminal patient, then analysts are the doctors and the LTV bankruptcy was the bitter pill that has instilled some discipline in this market.

The history of the high-yield markets is one of continual innovation. Recently, these innovations have included the creation of a security characterized as a bond that is actually equity-like in the sense that it is backed by very few assets, has deep subordination and low seniority, and is equity-like in its price fluctuations—responding to issuer developments rather than interest-rate fluctuations. Another innovation is the customizing of financial transactions to fit the economics of the issuing company and the needs of the buyer, as typified by zero-coupon bonds that gives the issuer time to implement a new strategy without the burden of cash payments.

Pike then turns to examine the historical record for high-yield bonds. He observes that realized returns have been high in comparison with returns on other types of fixed-income securities. On the other hand, the volatility of returns from high-yield bonds has been substantially lower than the volatility of returns from equities, and roughly in line with those of other fixed-income securities. While default rates have sometimes been high, they have not been so great as to erase the return advantage of the high-yield securities. He believes that these superior returns will persist as long as these securities are controversial. As he says, when everyone loves high-grade bonds it will be time to sell, but we have not yet reached that point.

Pike makes the distinction between junk bonds (issues near or in default that trade at large discounts from par) and high-income bonds (issues that are not in default and are not expected to go into default, even though their risk is greater than that of high-grade bonds). He estimates that the high-income market, which represented about 5 percent of the total taxable fixed-income corporate market in 1980, now accounts for 20 to 25 percent of that market. This broadening means that there are more issues and more opportunity for diversification, but it also means that performance of individual portfolios will be more dispersed and that investment analysis is more important.

Looking to the future, Pike sees secondary portfolios—characterized by poorer credit research and investment judgement—underperforming better-managed portfolios by substantial margins. Moreover, he concedes that in a depression scenario, high-income bonds would underperform the high-grade bond market, but would still substantially outperform the equity market. In a more positive vein, he feels that the high-yield bond market shows signs of increasing maturity, including more institutional participation with increased cash reserves, and that these developments should add an element of stability.

Pike concludes with some observations about the appropriateness of high-income bonds for institutional investors. First, these issues afford an opportunity to generate above-average returns. Second, the risk, as measured by return volatility, is limited. Third, liquidity has improved dramatically. Fourth, large household names have begun to appear in this market. For these reasons, he believes that a well-researched, diversified portfolio of high-yield bonds will come to be viewed as a clear alternative to both stocks and bonds in well-balanced institutional portfolios.

THE REAL ADVANTAGES OF SYNTHETIC SECURITIES

This two-part session focuses on synthetic securities. In the first presentation, Michael Asay suggests that the two most substantial developments in asset-backed securities today are the securitization of assets other than mortgages, and the unbundling and rebundling of cash flows from mortgage instruments, loosely described as synthetic securities. The motivation for the unbundling and rebundling is the inherent unpredictability of the cash flows from traditional fixed-rate mortgages. Taking the flows apart and repackaging them ideally leads to more predictable cash flows, but at a minimum it concentrates the uncertainty in ways that are more readily understood. This concentration is possible because of the well-known tendency for mortgages to have predictably different patterns of repayment at different interest-rate levels. This process has resulted in two types of securities: mortgage-backed strips consisting of interest-only and principal-only components, and collateralized mortgage obligations (CMOs). In his discussion, Asay emphasizes strips. The second part of the session, presented by Michael Youngblood, addresses CMOs.

Asay shows that a number of transactions have taken a current coupon security and broken it into two classes by stripping a portion of the coupon off one class and assigning it to another, thereby creating a low-coupon discount class and a high-coupon premium class backed by the same underlying pool of mortgages. The discount security has the usual high duration of low-coupon securities, and thus it is appealing to persons expecting interest-rate declines. The potential for rapid increases in the rate of prepayment, compared to a conventional low-coupon pass-through, backed by low-rate mortgages, also increases the appeal of this security to those expecting rate declines. The premium security has the low duration usually associated with high coupons, but it lacks the high uncertainty about prepayments of the conventional high-coupon pass-through. Thus, it is attractive to defensive, highly risk-averse investors concerned about interest-rate increases.

Additional examples show that it is possible to use the interest-only and principal-only strips to create a security with virtually any coupon and prepayment characteristic desired. Variations may be created more cheaply by beginning with the underlying pass-through instrument and simply adding interest only or principal only to it to produce the desired profile.

Michael Youngblood discusses CMOs, concentrating on the so-called CMO equity. In the creation of CMOs, an underlying pool of mortgages is divided up to create sequential or subsequent bands of payment classes with different effective lives, called tranches. In today's market, there is arbitrage potential in creating CMOs, because the yield on the underlying mortgages exceeds the weighted average yields on the various tranches. Therefore, there will be value remaining in the CMO trust after satisfaction of the debt obligations associated with each tranche. Moreover, income will be earned on funds received on the mortgages but not yet distributed to the holders of the tranches. This residual cash flow and additional income are the source of the CMO equity. Some CMOs are overcollateralized, and this also contributes to CMO equity.

According to Youngblood, CMO equity has three attractive attributes: impeccable quality, high cash-flow yields, and short effective lives. Its drawback is a vulnerability to changes in interest rates and prepayment rates that leads to a high standard deviation of returns across different interest-rate environments. The attractiveness of CMO equity arises from its ability to produce a bullish pattern of returns, similar to a principal-only strip; a bearish pattern of returns, similar to an interest-only strip; and a neutral pattern that provides high yields unless interest rates move dramatically lower or higher.

Analysis of the relationship between interest-rate levels and returns on CMO equity is complex indeed. It is possible, however, to get some sense of the forces at work by considering what happens to the CMO equity in the case of a fixed-rate CMO. For such a CMO, most of the arbitrage potential and the ability to earn income on temporary cash balances is associated with the shortest tranche, usually called the A tranche. This is because this tranche normally carries the lowest yields in comparison with the underlying mortgages. In high-interest-rate environments, the A tranche will survive longer due to low prepayments, increasing the period over which the arbitrage profits are earned. Moreover, high interest rates will increase the return on idle funds. Thus, the CMO equity will do very well in a high-interest-rate environment. On the other hand, in a low-interest-rate environment the A tranche is paid off quickly; income earned on idle balances is low, and thus the overall return to equity is low. Therefore, the value of the equity in a fixed-rate CMO will behave the same as an interest-only strip, rising in bear bond markets and falling in bull bond markets.

LINKED-DEBT INSTRUMENTS IN INSTITUTIONAL PORTFOLIOS

This session presents two perspectives on linked-debt instruments in institutional portfolios. First, Joel Miller discusses the topic from the viewpoint of an intermediary in the linked-debt instrument market. Rodney Gray follows with a presentation on a specific proposal for a petroleum-linked bond from the perspective of a corporate treasurer.

Linked-debt instruments are securities on which payoffs are related to the price performance of some underlying asset, such as gold, petroleum, currencies, or stock market indexes. Miller points out that such securities have existed in the past, especially when the linkage was to the price of gold. Today, the linkage is being offered as a way to control price risk, whereas in the past the linkage was probably a response to credit concerns.

Asset-linked securities serve two purposes. First, in contrast with conventionally-traded options and futures on assets, they allow issuers and investors to establish positions in assets that are customized to meet particular needs. For example, they have the effect of allowing investors to establish positions in assets for terms to expiration that far exceed those currently traded on exchanges. Second, they permit investors who are precluded from investing directly in assets, or options or futures on assets, to gain exposure indirectly to the assets' price fluctuations. In this way investors who could not otherwise hedge risk or otherwise modify their risk-return profiles may do so.

Important considerations in investing in asset-linked securities include credit, taxation and other legal issues, and the nature of the exposure that is assumed. According to Miller, it may be quite difficult to gather information on such securities. They also suffer from lack of accepted pricing methodologies, and this deficiency may lead to mispricing, reduced liquidity, and damaged market confidence.

Miller concludes his remarks with a review of three asset-linked bonds and how they have fared in the marketplace. He reviews a Sunshine Mining bond that was effectively convertible into silver, a French government bond that was tied to the price of gold and to the value of the dollar (because gold is priced in dollars), and a Standard Oil Company note indexed to the price of petroleum.

Rodney Gray's presentation illustrates Transco Energy Company's analysis of a proposal for a petroleum-linked bond that was presented to them in 1986. The proposed issue was for a five-year note with a yield that was 115 basis points over the Treasury rate and was effectively convertible into petroleum at $20 per barrel at the option of the investor, with the investor exercising by putting the security to Transco. The company elected not to issue the proposed security, and in the process of explaining this decision Gray provides some insights into the potential for and the drawbacks of such securities.

With respect to cost, the yield was attractive compared to the company's conventional borrowing rates. On the other hand, the conversion price seemed low in an environment in which oil was selling at $16 per barrel, and was expected by the company to reach $21 per barrel in a year or two. Because interest rates and petroleum prices tend to move together, there was a good chance that the issue would have to be refunded when rates were high. With respect to funding risk and flexibility, the issue was not attractive. It contained uncertainty with respect to both its cost and the timing of the payoff. Moreover, the issue was difficult to analyze, both alone and as a part of Transco's total liability portfolio. Finally, management felt that

it had other, more attractive financing alternatives.

In summary, Gray reports that management's preference would be for an issue that effectively reverses the direction of the oil price and interest-rate effects from those of the security Transco was offered, so that the cost of borrowing would be reduced when petroleum prices fall.

THE NEXT DECADE IN THE ECONOMY

In this session, Jay Forrester discusses his view of the economy over the next decade. Although his presentation is not directly related to innovation in fixed-income securities, the health of the economy over the next decade is of significant importance to the fixed-income market.

Forrester focuses on the existence of an economic long wave. In his view, the 1920s are analogous to present times. Some parallels include high real interest rates, low growth in real wages, declining prices of agricultural land, a high rate of bank failures, high levels of merger and acquisition activity, foreign debt problems, and a "get-rich-quick" syndrome. His best estimate is that the long wave peaked in the late 1970s and that the low point will be in the mid-1990s. Therefore, at this time we are experiencing a long-wave downturn.

This analysis leads to a forecast of possible deflation, although Forrester notes that it is possible to have a physical depression accompanied by inflation. In any event, there will be underutilization of manufacturing capacity and rising unemployment. Forrester believes that in time, these influences will affect the financial markets, with adverse consequences.

INDEXING FIXED-INCOME INVESTMENTS

Rick Nelson discusses the evolution of bond indexing, the current level of activity, index selection, and trading techniques to create an index fund and enhance its performance.

Indexation of bond portfolios is largely a phenomenon of the 1980s. Its evolution has been heavily influenced by the move toward passive portfolio management in the equity asset management field. Before 1981, the greater precision techniques such as immunization and dedication absorbed much of the demand for bond indexing. Since that time, activity has grown to approximately $30 billion in straight indexation, with another $20 billion in customized or enhanced-return index funds. In contrast, dedicated and immunized portfolios still account for over $100 billion.

According to Nelson, bond indexation makes sense for three reasons. First, it provides a structured approach to investment in the fixed-income market; second, it is cheaper than active management; and third, index performance has historically compared well with the results of active management.

There are also two arguments against indexing. It is difficult to assert that a bond market index represents an efficient portfolio. Moreover, it may be that none of the standard bond indexes reflect a portfolio strategy or return pattern that investors really desire. For example, it is well understood that rising interest rates reduce effective bond durations. Therefore, an indexed portfolio will tend toward a shorter duration when rates rise, just when many investors might want to maintain or increase their interest-rate exposure. The converse effect will prevail in a declining rate environment, producing longer durations just when many investors desire less interest-rate exposure.

There are two factors involved in choosing an index: the components of the index and the source of the index values. In some instances, it may be appropriate to bypass the broad published bond market indexes and to concentrate instead on the subindexes. In this way, the indexed portfolio may be structured to fit the needs of the investor or the overall investment strategy more closely than would a portfolio structured along the lines of a broad market index. With respect to the second issue, it might be argued that some sources provide better prices than others. The major indexes, however, appear to track each other closely.

Once an appropriate index or package of indexes is chosen, the task of structuring an actual portfolio remains. Two approaches to portfolio design are used. One involves stratified sampling, in which individual securities are incorporated in the portfolio so that the proportionate representation of different characteristics corresponds to their weighting in the index. This approach has the advantage of being independent of historical returns, but with several dimensions it may be complex and require a large number of bonds to implement. Another alternative, which Nelson calls a "risk model" approach, involves identifying the factors that are important to bond risk and return and evaluating how the index relates to them. Individual security issues are then chosen to minimize index tracking errors while maximizing yield. This approach is operative with a smaller number of issues, and it permits some risk-return trade-off. It suffers, however, from being dependent on historical data and from errors in the estimates that are employed.

Nelson notes that value may be added to the indexed portfolio through pricing and trading style decisions, as well as through swaps and similar activities. The natural extension of this activity is to "enhanced" index funds, where an active management is employed within the context of client-defined constraints on portfolio composition.

SECURITIZATION STRATEGIES

Securitization involves taking financial assets that have no public market, such as receivables, and converting them into securities that are tradeable in secondary markets. According to Anthony Dub, the issuance of asset-backed securities by industrial corporations is comparatively new, having begun in 1985. Because the amount of consumer and other installment debt outstanding is large, the potential for this activity is great. Moreover, because the life of the assets is typically short, there is potential for a high volume of originations; this is attractive to investment bankers.

Companies securitize assets for three reasons. First, it is an additional way of providing funds to support assets. Second, it provides an ultimate response to the problems of matching assets and liabilities by allowing the liability to follow the asset directly. Third, it may be cheaper than issuance of conventional debt securities, especially when one considers that little or no equity is needed to support asset-backed securities.

Ideal assets for securitization have predictable cash flows, intrinsically high quality, and a life exceeding one year. For example, Dub observes that automobile receivables meet all of these criteria, as most people make their payments regularly, the underlying physical asset is readily marketable at a price that usually exceeds the amount of the receivable, and the initial term is for several years.

Dub concludes with a discussion of three aspects of asset-backed securities that should be of interest to investors.

- *Credit quality.* Credit quality is high because of the quality of the underlying asset, and because many asset-backed securities have credit enhancement features, including recourse to the issuer, reserve funds, and backing by letters of credit or surety bonds. Moreover, asset-backed securities are free of so-called event risk, which arises when a bond issuer subsequently takes some action that diminishes the quality of the promise. For these reasons, all asset-backed securities to date have carried AAA or AA agency ratings.
- *Consistent prepayment experience.* In both absolute terms and comparison with mortgage-related securities, asset-backed securities have little prepayment risk. Moreover, prepayments tend to be independent of the level of interest rates. For example, while people may prepay their automobile loans for various reasons, they rarely do so to refinance at lower interest rates.
- *High yields.* At this time, asset-backed securities sell at higher yield premia over equivalent-maturity Treasury securities than do comparable conventional bonds. According to Dub, the principal reason is that people do not understand the asset-backed securities well, and they are unfamiliar with the trading characteristics of this market.

OPPORTUNITIES IN GLOBALIZATION

Michael Ivanovitch begins this session with the observation that transnational money and capital market operations are anything but new. What distinguishes recent activity is the pace of global portfolio diversification and the extent to which all major segments of financial markets have become more integrated internationally. While British investors have traditionally led in international investment, the United States and Japan are currently the most prominent participants.

International asset holdings of United States, United Kingdom, and Japanese pension funds are estimated to have expanded two to three times as fast as their domestic components in the first six year of this decade. Some observers expect that by the early 1990s about $300 billion, or 8 percent of total pension fund assets, will be invested internationally. One result is greatly increased foreign participation in major equity securities markets. Eurocurrency and currency trading have also become important global markets in recent years.

A complex interaction of public policies, markets, and technological advances has been the main force behind this internationalization. The elimination of capital controls and restrictions on the activities of foreign financial institutions have been major forces, as have large budget deficits in most industrial countries. Financial innovations have widened the choice of investments; at the same time, they have made it easier to control risk and have increased liquidity. Recognition of the portfolio diversification gains from international investment has also played a large role, as have advances in information processing and transmission.

Ivanovitch feels that this pace of globalization will continue. In addition to the continuing impact of the factors that have been the main forces behind globalization, two other developments will be important. One is the increased pool of investment outlets due to privatization programs in industrialized countries and debt-equity conversions in the developing world. The other is the increased demand for financial assets due to the growth of mutual funds that have attracted small savers to the stock and bond markets, the demographic and economic conditions in many countries that have led to rapid growth of pension funds and other retirement arrangements, and other occurrences that have increased the world pool of savings. All these developments suggest that globalization of financial transactions is a deeply rooted and irreversible process rather than a passing fad.

Ivanovitch next offers a brief review of the economic outlook for the major western nations of the world. He sees a picture emerging for economic activity in these countries that includes slow growth, declining credit demand, and generally subdued inflationary pressure. Ideally, large financial imbalances would lead to significant policy shifts, such as fiscal contraction in the United States; but as a practical matter, Ivanovitch feels that much of the compensation will have to be made by the markets through exchange-rate induced impacts on economic activity and total asset returns. This means that the dollar will continue to decline until there is convincing evidence of a turnaround in U.S. trade accounts, and more expansionary fiscal and monetary policies in major surplus countries. The expected easing of credit conditions outside the United States bodes well for foreign bond markets. Equity markets may be more treacherous because of slower growth and falling profits, and because in a number of cases, share prices have been run up due to changes in regulation and shifts in investment patterns rather than major shifts in the outlook for economic growth and corporate earnings.

THE FEDERAL RESERVE'S VIEW OF INNOVATIVE SECURITIES

The concluding speaker on the program was Paul Volcker, then chairman of the Federal Reserve Board. Although it was not known at the time of the seminar, these were the last days of Volcker's second term; he was to resign his position shortly afterward. Volcker's remarks are well worth reading because they provide a sense of the man, and because much of his message has always been in his manner of delivery—what he does not say as well as what he says. Volcker's presentation includes both prepared remarks and an extensive question and answer session.

Emphasizing that the Federal Reserve System does not have an institutional view of innovative securities, Volcker outlined several of his concerns regarding the development of these securities.

- Many innovative securities have the potential to improve people's situations by allowing risks to be redistributed. There is a danger, however, that in the process some risks may be aggravated. It is important to realize that many real risks simply cannot be eliminated, only transferred.

- Until we better understand what may happen with the new securities forms under adverse market circumstances, caution is warranted in their use.

- There is a danger that some of the new instruments may encourage speculation.

- Some of these instruments are not all that new; for example, mortgage bonds that looked a great deal like mortgage-backed securities were available in the 1920s. The ultimate experience with them was not a happy one.

- International debt is currently a major problem area, and it is possible that the volume of international lending has been excessive. The problem, however, is more manageable than it was four or five years ago. By and large the debt burden has declined relative to the ability to service it. Many countries with large debt problems have undertaken economic policy measures that are favorable for the long run—moving toward more liberal treatment of business with an outward-looking direction that is less state dominated. It is probably better that international debts not be securitized, as some have suggested, because the problems associated with these debts can be managed better in the banking system.

Opening Remarks

Delores S. Driscoll, CFA

A few years ago, investment professionals receiving an invitation to a conference titled "Innovations in Fixed-Income Instruments and Markets" might have assumed that there had been a typographical error. The bond market was hardly a reservoir of creative new ideas. In fact, many of us can remember when managing bonds meant plotting the daily price patterns of the Treasury 4.25s of 1992 as their yields fluctuated violently between 4 and 4.5 percent. Today, by contrast, bond investors face a dizzying menu of instruments in which to invest. In 1986, one investment house published not less than 48 separate bond indexes. Investors now can choose from a universe of collateralized securities of all possible descriptions, including variable-rate notes, international bonds, bonds with imbedded put and call options on various commodities, and recently, mortgages which have been stripped into interest-only and principal-only pieces. It is enough to make an equity investor's job look easy.

Clearly, the progressive deregulation of the banking and financial system has been an important factor in bringing about this explosion of innovation in the U.S. bond market. From deregulation has emerged what investment professionals have labeled *liability primacy management*. The average maturity of savings institution liabilities has shortened and become market sensitive, triggering securitization in unprecedented amounts and myriad new forms.

Another key factor has been the restructuring of corporate America. While financial institutions have been adjusting their portfolios, the corporate sector has been cutting and pasting its balance sheet and income statement. The inevitable by-product has been the emergence and rapid growth of the high-yield or junk sector of the bond market. Along with securitization, this must rank as one of the most significant innovations in recent U.S. history.

The third issue, globalization, has two elements: currency volatility and a heightened awareness of the importance of world markets. Together, they have encouraged expansion in the international markets. Today it is routine to issue, buy, sell, and hedge a variety of bonds in a multitude of currencies in markets throughout the world. Instantaneous global communication, intense computerization, and education all facilitate this innovative trend.

Finally, competition has had a significant impact on innovation in the fixed-income markets. Financial assets have returned to popularity at the expense of real assets in the disinflationary environment of the 1980s. The ranks of dealers and underwriters have swelled. They are intelligent and creative, and they know that whoever creates a successful new instrument will be rewarded well. Meanwhile, performance sensitivity has intensified dramatically, which has encouraged money managers to be bold and innovative, holding forth the prospects of enhanced return or more closely controlled risk. In sum, we have seen a revolution which has dramatically altered our financial universe and our tasks as portfolio managers and analysts. The result is an exciting investment environment.

What are the implications of innovation? Economist Jay Forrester of the Massachusetts Institute of Technology (MIT) perceives that the volatility of today's financial market is symptomatic of the late stages of the economic long-wave cycle.[1] On a somewhat happier note, innovation certainly breeds excitement. There are expanded opportunities to make or lose money for clients. There is an even greater need for a fertile, bottom-line research focus on the details. I believe that a careful analysis of many recent innovative bond instruments suggests a spurious benefit and a high imbedded cost to the buyer—reflecting my contrarian instincts.

Innovation is risky business; its absence also is risky business. For example, in 1986, when Treasury bills returned 6.5 percent and long strips 69 percent, no prudent investor could fail to see that with new opportunities come vastly-expanded risk horizons and the risks of under-

[1] See Professor Forrester's presentation, pp. 42–54

performance, either by acts of omission or commission.

I would like to conclude with a historical note. We may think that financial innovation is a 1980s phenomenon. In fact, in seventeenth-century England, a man named Samuel Pepys—financier to the King's Navy—devised and used many of the same innovative concepts that were supposed to have been invented or discovered recently by Wall Street's best and brightest.

Innovations in Perspective

Brian F. Wruble, CFA

Financial innovation has always existed. The introduction of currency in place of barter is an obvious example of innovation. The topic of financial innovations is particularly interesting at the present time because of the explosion of innovations in the fixed-income market.

Innovation deals with the essence of financial transactions and changes in the way these transactions are structured. Financial transactions involve bringing together buyers and sellers of real, financial, or intangible assets in a way that both buyer and seller feel is helpful. Transactions can take place only when those on either side have different needs. This is the fundamental building block of all commerce—or for that matter, all human interaction. In the process, value is created because the utility of the transacting parties increases. Financial innovation allows players in the market to concentrate on what they do well, and shed activities and their associated risks where they cannot do as well.

FINANCIAL INNOVATION: THE SAVINGS AND LOAN EXAMPLE

The securitization of mortgages is a great example of financial innovation. The local savings and loan, with its strong community franchise, is exceedingly well-equipped to originate traditional fixed-rate mortgages in its own community. It can assess the creditworthiness of the borrower, appraise the property, and do the paperwork. On the other hand, savings and loans are not nearly as well-positioned to hold fixed-rate mortgages because of their deposit base of relatively short-term liabilities.

Return on capital for a savings and loan comes from two activities: originating and servicing mortgages and acting as a financial intermediary—financing new mortgages with its deposit base. The first activity has low risk but high value added. The savings and loan has a strong local franchise and natural competitive advantages. In most cases, a nonlocal partici-

pant faces real competitive barriers in originating mortgages.

The second activity is far more risky. The inherent asset/liability mismatch puts the savings and loan's capital at risk, and the return on capital probably is not high enough in the intermediation activities to justify this risk. Financial markets do not pay participants to bear risks that can be shed. Through the securitization innovation, however, savings and loans can package and securitize mortgages and sell them, enabling them to focus on their origination capability, and pass the risk of holding long assets on to those who have long liabilities.

An alternative financial innovation for savings and loans is the adjustable-rate mortgage. Adjustable-rate mortgages allow savings and loans to pass on the interest-rate risk to borrowers.

Because of these financial innovations, savings and loans now have choices. They may choose the business that they want to be in and how to add value. They also may decide what risks they want to take, which of those risks the market will pay for, which may be shed, and, given rapidly increasing efficiency, which ones *should* be shed, since the markets will not pay for all risks.

CATALYST FOR INNOVATION

The array of new instruments available to investors and to users of capital has expanded enormously in the past several years. Today there are CATs (Certificate of Accrual on Treasury Securities), TIGERs (Treasury Investors Growth Receipts), and CMOs (Collateralized Mortgage Obligations). Futures are available on Treasury bills, Eurodollar deposits, Treasury notes, bonds, Ginnie Maes, stock indexes, foreign currencies, and the Consumer Price Index. There are options on many of those futures, as well as on the underlying cash instruments. Interest-rate swaps and currency swaps can be constructed also along with interest-rate protection agreements such as caps and floors and collars and windows.

The pace of financial innovation has accelerated for three reasons. First, the world has become more dangerous. Increased volatility is a key motivation for financial innovation. Intermediaries tend to operate by holding relatively large assets that are financed by relatively large liabilities. The difference between these two large numbers is a rather small number—capital—which means that volatility of either assets or liabilities has a leveraged effect on capital. Increased volatility in markets has a tremendous impact on both the downside and the upside for the intermediary, sharply reducing the intermediary's ability to control its future. This has forced investors to understand the risks they are taking. With greater volatility, there is an increased penalty for making the wrong decisions.

Second, given this greater volatility, market participants have become more self-aware. Investors must ask themselves what they really want and where they can add value; they must question their appetite for risk.

Third, the resources needed by decision-makers to analyze these issues have reached a critical mass. These resources are as diverse as the Black-Scholes Option Pricing Model, the personal computer, the Concorde aircraft, and satellite transmission of data to financial markets around the globe.

Professor Jay Forrester of MIT has designed an economic model which has helped many investment professionals gain perspective on the very long-term processes of our economy.[1] One of the observations made by Professor Forrester and his team is that there is a distinction between invention and innovation. Inventions tend to occur randomly over time, while innovations are the industries that spring up to use the inventions. Major innovation seems to cluster around infrequent and widely-spaced periods of creative economic destruction and renewal. In other words, there are always many good ideas around, but it takes a period of real change and stress to bring to bear the critical mass of resources necessary for innovation.

The burst of financial market innovation seems to fit this model. A critical mass has been achieved. The stresses of the late 1970s and the early 1980s shook the world's financial intermediaries. The financial inventions of the past decade or so were waiting to be applied. The values to be captured were so great that the financial services industry was able to hire the best and the brightest to seek new ways to facilitate transactions.

INNOVATION: SOME EXAMPLES

These innovations are being used more and more frequently in the financial services industry. Equitable Capital, for example, manages billions of dollars in assets, consisting of publicly-traded common stocks, privately-placed bonds, cash instruments, venture capital, and leveraged buyouts. Each of the firm's portfolios has its own objectives and purposes. Some of the portfolios—performance primacy portfolios—are designed to squeeze out all the performance possible within specific beta or duration constraints. Others, such as liability primacy portfolios, are intended to backstop specific pools of liabilities, enabling the firm to meet client obligations and still earn a profit. The use of specialized instruments has become widespread and absolutely essential in the management of these assets.

The high-yield bond market is a marvelous example of innovation that rose to meet the economy's need for regeneration. The ability of less creditworthy issuers to obtain financing to restructure corporations has released an enormous amount of value. It has helped to make clusters of economic activity—whole companies or divisions of companies—more freely tradeable. When high-yield bonds are used to finance a leveraged buyout, there is a decrease in the risks associated with entrenched management operating in their own interests and being mesmerized by short-term measures. These risks are traded off for financial risk—the risk of high leverage. This risk, embodied in 10 to 1 leverage ratios, for example, with high-yield bonds at the bottom of the capitalization structure, is distributed broadly across institutions and across the public in a diversifiable form. Over time, as the leveraged buyout works out, that leverage risk is reduced. The resulting corporation is a leaner, more efficient entity, better able to meet the utility preferences of its owners, lenders, customers, and employees. The leveraged buyout may be one of this generation's responses to the

---

[1] See Professor Forrester's presentation, pp. 42–54.

kinds of financial stress that were dealt with badly during the 1930s.

The basic inventions that fuel a wave of innovation are able to benefit both parties involved in a transaction. The development of mutual funds is a good example. Mutual funds brought professional asset management services to the public. The providers of mutual funds, in turn, achieved the scale of assets under management and fees needed to support high-powered research staff, skilled portfolio managers, and a great deal of advertising. Both sides of this transaction perceive that they have benefited.

In the past 10 years, individual inventions have clustered into a wave of innovation driven by a sharp increase in global market awareness by all involved in these markets. Financial deregulation has put them into each others' businesses, which in turn has forced them to take a closer look at their own businesses and to determine what business they actually are in.

The innovation wave has brought greatly increased efficiency. The availability of technology, whether it be global communications or personal computers, has supported the process of innovation. The high pace of change has resulted in the creation and redistribution of wealth. When wealth is created and redistributed on a massive scale, considerable human capital is attracted to the process. This process is fueled by the kind of brain power and energy that accompanied the great innovative waves in other industries.

For the fixed-income practitioner, innovations might be grouped into four categories. The first group is cash market innovations, including stripped Treasury instruments such as CATs and TIGERs; asset-backed securities such as CMOs; putable and extendable securities; floating-rate securities, some with caps and floors; and high-yield bonds. The second group is derivative market innovations: futures on financial instruments; futures on the S&P 500 Index or Consumer Price Index and options on those futures; futures on fixed-income cash instruments; interest-rate swaps; currency swaps; and interest-rate protection agreements such as caps, floors, collars, and windows. The third group involves new management strategies such as greater emphasis by intermediaries on asset/liability management; hedging; dynamic asset allocation or portfolio insurance; covered call writing; the creation of synthetic assets; program trading; immunization and contingent immunization; dedication; indexation; and the leveraged recapitalization or buyout. The fourth relates to the introduction and use of new analytics: duration; the concept of convexity; the ability to assess prepayment risks, particularly on mortgage-backed instruments; option valuation techniques; and improved techniques for valuing all kinds of securities as well as the supporting technology.

Financial innovations are created by a number of very smart people drawn to the excitement and rewards that accompany periods of great change in the marketplace. The tremendous array of new resources available to providers of capital, intermediaries, and users of capital is a sign of great vitality in our capital markets.

Question and Answer Session

QUESTION: Please expand on the discrepancy between your comment that there is high value through innovation and Ms. Driscoll's comment that there may be high imbedded costs?

WRUBLE: It is clear to me that any time a transaction meets the needs of both parties, value is added, or the transaction would not take place. The pace of transactions has increased enormously. Each transaction adds value on both sides through efficiency increases or friction reduction—that must be adding to wealth in the aggregate. There are costs which must also be considered, however: people are employed; machines are employed; telephone lines are used in each of these transactions.

QUESTION: Volatility in bonds has dropped dramatically. Will the pace of innovation decelerate?

WRUBLE: There are many theories on why volatility has dropped. It is a relatively short-run phenomenon. Recently people have noticed that the bond markets have been quiet. One point of view is that this may be the beginning of the next bear market in bonds. That is the way most bear markets start, when nobody is looking and things get quiet. But it is very hard to imagine anybody saying they will eschew the use of interest-rate futures because they do not see an opportunity to use them. It just does not seem reasonable.

QUESTION: Is innovation eliminating the need for serious research on companies?

WRUBLE: No, I feel very strongly that research is still important. I believe that markets are relatively efficient and that they become somewhat more efficient through innovative securities, but that there are always inefficiencies. It is a big world out there; thus a corner always exists where someone can find value. Fundamental research will not disappear. The minute it does, opportunities will be popping up all over the place for the one person who wants to continue doing fundamental research. I would love to be that person.

QUESTION: You assert that businesses are not paid for risks that they can shed. Isn't the risk that is shed assumed by someone else?

WRUBLE: That is *not* correct. The S&L example underscores my point. S&Ls operating in a vacuum as they once did, with long fixed-rate mortgages and short-term deposits, were in fact performing a function in the economy and they were getting paid for it, but they got brutally punished every few years when the yield curve inverted. There are plenty of people out there with long-term liabilities and an appetite for long-term assets. Once someone figured out how to package the S&L's long-term assets and sell them to people who could match them on their balance sheet, the risk of both players was reduced. Once that door was opened, it is hard for me to conceive that either player would continue to get paid for holding that risk.

The High-Yield Bond Market—Part I

James Grant

These are most peculiar and interesting times for the bond market. In the past year, there have been record numbers of corporate bond downgrades, corporate bond defaults, bank failures, personal bankruptcies, and federal agencies which are essentially bankrupt. From my perspective, credit is sick. It is as if a wonderfully-restored Victorian home is opened up for the first viewing and people are ushered in, marvelling at the lavish and tasteful furnishings, the wonderful paint job, and the woodwork faithfully restored. Finally, they get down to business and begin bidding for the home in subtle, polite ways, gradually upping the ante, when suddenly someone comes up from the basement and says, "I didn't want to tell you, but there are termites down there." Everyone looks at this person and thinks, "Who are you, and what do you mean? Go away." And the bidding continues.

The market seems to be in that phase now. Using the Victorian house analogy, there are termites in the house of credit. I believe, however, that the termites can be fumigated, possibly through something that might be called "equitization". If the stock market continues to rise, companies that are highly leveraged, such as Texas Air, might show a stronger balance sheet if they can sell stock. These companies might not otherwise be able to weather the next recession.

It should be noted that the junk bond market is not as big as some have suggested. It is worth approximately $100 billion—or about the equivalent of the debt that Brazil owes but might not pay. Alternatively, it is approximately one-third of the market capitalization of Nippon Telegraph and Telephone. It is only five times larger than the perpetual floating-rate note market in London that went out of business because one Wednesday morning in December, no one wanted perpetual floating-rate notes. It is not an enormous market. What makes it interesting and worthy of study, even for those not involved directly, is how it might be symptomatic of the times, and how it might illustrate the credit cycle.

The concept of the credit cycle comes from research following the Great Depression. In the mid to late 1930s, the National Bureau of Economic Research commissioned a series of studies on what caused the Depression. That series makes very interesting reading now. Of particular interest is a report by Ilse Mintz.[1] Mintz examined the high-yield market of the 1920s, which basically was the market in sovereign-funded debt. At the time, the government market was yielding around 4 percent and these bonds were yielding 6.5 to 7 percent. So the spread between junk bonds and government issues was very much like it is today.

What happened to that market is most revealing. The sale of such sovereign-funded debt began, haltingly, in the early 1920s. There was a great deal of skepticism about it. After all, the United States had just been through a major debt liquidation. People felt that high-yield issues were risky. Nevertheless, the innovators were rewarded, and this gave rise to imitators. Many countries, such as the Austro-Hungarian empire, Brazil, Bolivia, and Peru became major issuers of high-yield debt.

An interesting thing happened during that period. Credit quality deteriorated as the decade wore on. Mintz studied the rates of default in the aftermath of the break in 1929 and 1930, and discovered that securities issued earlier in the boom had a relatively good track record, whereas securities issued late, in the manic end of the boom, had a very high incidence of default. Her hypothesis was that, just like a boxer who gets cocky in the late rounds and drops his left, so the market drops its guard. Standards of due diligence decline. If the market goes up, it only serves to verify the good opinions. One thing leads to another, and suddenly people are not reading prospectuses, if they

[1]Mintz, Ilse, "Deterioration in the Quality of Foreign Bonds Issued in the United States: 1920 to 1930," *National Bureau of Economic Research*, 1951.

even get them. The result is that lower-quality credits come to market on terms that increasingly do not compensate investors for the risks they bear.

Interestingly, the same results came to light in studies of other securities markets of that period, such as commercial real estate, residential real estate, and corporate debt. The later in the cycle the securities were issued, the higher the subsequent rate of default. A very imprecise way to think of the credit cycle is that it begins with skepticism and ends with a kind of manic optimism. There is no telling where one is in the cycle, except perhaps through taking a sounding of contrary opinion, or reading prospectuses and deciding that it looks manic. This approach, however, does not always provide the right timing answer.

Within this framework, the top of the market is reached when a marginal investment banker reaching for fees shakes hands with a marginal investor reaching for yield. By marginal investment banker, I do not mean the least well-reputed or the least fashionable investment banker. I mean the investment banker who is the hungriest, who insists on buying market share, perhaps through a lack of due diligence or a lack of scruples, and therefore tolerates lower standards of coverage than might otherwise be acceptable. The recent Allied Stores prospectus provides an example. The deal was so successful that it had to be expanded in size, and the yields were only about 400 basis points more than Macy's was obliged to pay only a year earlier. The comfort and coverage margins on the deal, however, are remarkable only for their thinness. More to the point, I am struck by the significance of First Boston electing to take about $850 million worth of that deal onto its balance sheet—a balance sheet showing net worth of less than $1 billion. What does that tell us about where we are in the credit cycle, when a very thinly-structured deal sounds so good that even the brokers like it?

Nonetheless, the First Boston-Allied Stores episode reveals an attitude in the market; an attitude of credulity, faith, conviction, and optimism. People do not seem to be evaluating whether we are rejecting enough of these deals, and whether we are giving the investors the comfort and the coverage they should get. Instead, people seem to be saying, "Let's step up and take a shot."

My favorite high-yield market datum comes from the Merrill-Lynch office in Boston. It is the reading of the portfolio composition of high-yield mutual funds. The balance sheet shows that in 1982, the percentage of assets in these funds rated B or less, or not rated at all, was about 48 percent. That is a component of these funds that might be called sub-junk. At last report, the percentage of assets rated B or less, or not rated at all, was 74 percent. Investment bankers are out there reaching for fees; investment managers are reaching for yield. I am not sure when risk begins to eclipse reward, but I certainly believe that we are getting closer than we ever have been before.

The High-Yield Bond Market—Part II

William H. Pike, CFA

I would like to begin with an observation: if credit is sick and high-income bonds are the terminal patient, then analysts are the doctors and LTV was the bitter pill.[1] The bankruptcy of LTV put some credit discipline back in the market. Immediately following that bankruptcy, the market went down; but when it recovered, only the better credits in the industry recovered. The poorer credits remained depressed, and this tended to move them into those portfolios which were most able to accept that risk. The latter is a favorable development in this industry.

INNOVATION IN THE HIGH-YIELD BOND MARKET

The proceedings of this conference seem to involve two topics: the first is innovation, and the second is an assessment of risk. The history of the high-income market has been one of continual innovation, and there are two particular innovations that are worth mentioning. First, an equity-like product which is masked as a bond has been created; and second, financial transactions have been customized to fit the economics of the issuing company and the needs of the buyer.

I make a distinction between the word *bond*, which implies there is an asset backing the issue, and *debenture*, which is issued against the full faith in credit of the company. High-income bonds look like equity because they are debentures; they are not really bonds. To the extent that high-income issues are marginal credits, there is very little property of value behind these issues. Second, high-income bonds usually are deeply subordinated and have low seniority, if any, in the event of a reorganization. Banks and senior lenders usually have the right to stop payments on subordinated issues for six to nine months in the event of a technical default to the senior lenders and the right to prevent acceleration for long periods of time.

[1] See Mr. Grant's presentation, pp. 16–17.

The trustee may have the right to delay notification of default. Thus, senior lenders can negotiate their position in reorganization with almost complete disregard for the interests of high-income bondholders. For these reasons, high-income bonds look like equity.

The price behavior of high-income bonds, both on the upside and the downside, often is more like equity than high-grade bonds. Even some secured bonds behave like equity. For example, when People's Express had problems during the summer of 1986, their secured bonds temporarily declined 30 to 40 percent. On the upside, occasionally I have seen high-income bonds move 10 to 30 percent on news of takeovers, asset sales, earnings breakouts—basically the same features that move equities. The equity-like characteristics of high-yield bonds drive both variability and return in the high-income market. For that reason, equity-type analysis and risk assessment techniques have become important in the high-income bond market.

The biggest difference between equity and high-income bonds is that most of the return on equity is in the future, whereas bonds get a coupon every six months. The coupon may be reinvested for the compounding benefits. Thus, high-income bonds really are equity masked as bonds. The mask, of course, is the coupon, some covenant protection—which is unimpressive but beginning to improve—and finally, some security.

It is important to distinguish between high-income and junk bonds. In my view, junk implies issues which are in default, very near default, or widely expected to go into default. Junk bonds trade as low as 20 to 50 cents on the dollar. High-income bonds, in contrast, are those which are not in default and are not expected to go into default, although they have a higher risk of subsequently going into default than high-grade bonds.

The second innovation in the high-yield market is the custom tailoring of the product. The most obvious example is the zero coupon issue. High-grade zero coupon bonds existed before high-income zeros, but their purpose was different. The primary purpose of high-grade zero coupon bonds was to conserve cash, or to try to match the repayment of the bond with cash flows. Low-grade zeros usually are issued to reflect a specific purpose. For example, in a restructuring or reorganization, management may want time to implement a new strategy without the burden of cash payments. This can be accomplished using zero coupon bonds or zero fixes—a zero coupon that switches to a coupon bond after two to five years.

Other examples of the custom tailoring of the product include payment-in-kind bonds, or PIKs, which pay their interest in the form of additional bonds for two to five years before switching to cash interest payments; PIK-preferreds; convertibles; exchangeables; and the springing-reset note. A springing-reset note was issued by LTV in early 1986. This bond was issued as a very junior issue because of an existing indenture restriction on another LTV bond issue. When that issue is repaid, eliminating the restriction, the springing-reset issue will spring up to a senior position, and its interest rate will reset. It has a very clever title, which made it easy to sell compared to other LTV securities; however, this feature in no way overcomes the problem of the credit risk of LTV in general. An example of tailoring the issue to the economics of the company is the increasing-rate note. The sooner management can accomplish its goals and retire the notes, the less it has to pay. Similarly, PIKs encourage management to reduce the amount of bonds or preferreds outstanding, since they compound the number of bonds and therefore the eventual cash interest the company will have to pay when the PIK converts to cash.

Another innovation is the participation note. Within the past two or three years, several companies have issued bonds which, in addition to their fixed coupon, pay an additional amount if the company's pretax earnings, or operating earnings, increase beyond a certain level. This participation enables the issuing company to pay a slightly lower fixed coupon than otherwise would be necessary to sell the issue.

In a macro sense, the high-income market took business away from the banks and insurance companies, which once were the primary lenders to high-risk companies. Historically,

banks and insurance companies have tended to straitjacket management with tight covenants. High-income bonds are far less burdensome. In 1981, for example, there were few covenants, and prospectuses were thin. Now, of course, prospectuses may be a quarter-inch thick, and covenants have increased. Nevertheless, management generally is offered far more flexibility in borrowing from issuers of high-income securities than by borrowing from banks and insurance companies.

The ultimate example of management flexibility is the blind pool, where money is lent with the promise that management will acquire something and do great things with it. That may not appear to be an intelligent way to invest, but many blind pools have been very successful.

Another innovative dimension of this market relates to the types of firms that have been able to obtain financing in the high-yield market that might otherwise have had great difficulty raising capital. For example, the gaming companies are financed by the high-yield market, as are many hostile takeovers, leveraged buyouts, and restructurings. Many of these companies have provided substantial returns to high-yield investors.

Not all investments are successful, however. Some of the high-risk oil companies are a good example. Crystal Oil, Global Marine, Kenai, and MGF are companies that issued high-yield debt in the early 1980s and subsequently defaulted.

ASSESSMENT OF RISK IN THE HIGH-YIELD BOND MARKET

In general, risk is viewed in terms of relative returns and the variability of such returns. I would like to review a few statistics on the six-year compounded growth rate of actual total returns across the fixed-income markets. First Boston's high-yield index ended 1986 with an 18.08 percent return. Fifty-two basis points behind that was the Shearson Lehman Corporate Index, followed by the Salomon Brothers mortgage pass-through at 17.39 percent, the Shearson Lehman Government Corporate at 16.06 percent, the Shearson Lehman Government Agency at 15.59 percent, and the S&P 500 at 15.30 percent. Similarly, the data shows that the volatility of returns for all of the fixed-income products was lower than the volatility of stocks, and that high income in particular was in the lower half of that spectrum. The statistics also show that the volatility of monthly returns was substantially lower in the high-yield market than for equities, and roughly in line with those of other fixed-income products.

Another way to look at risk is the default rate for this market. In 1982, the default rate was 3.6 percent; in 1983, it was 1 percent; in 1984, 0.8 percent; in 1985, 1.7 percent; and in 1986, 3 percent. All of these returns were accomplished despite the sometimes high default rate.

Is volatility a good measure of risk? Not necessarily. Some of our most creditworthy issues are the most volatile, but not for credit-related reasons. In addition, some high-income portfolios have performed quite well, but some have not, reflecting meaningful differences in credit research and investment judgment. In the next several years, I believe there will be greater dispersion of performance with much lower returns from the secondary portfolios because of defaults. Furthermore, I believe that in a 1930s depression scenario, high-income bonds would underperform the high-grade bond market, although they might still outperform the equity market substantially, even after adjusting for defaults. Short of a depression, however, I believe that the risks are reasonable and, as the record shows, are more than compensated for by the premium yields.

The high-income bond mutual funds have weathered bad news well. If one looked at a history of bond fund price fluctuations, it would be difficult to pick the day LTV went bankrupt. In the month following LTV's declaration of bankruptcy, the entire high-income market was very weak. Fidelity Management's high-income fund, which had a net asset value of $10 per share prior to the LTV bankruptcy, bottomed out one month later at $9.80. Within another month, the market was back to new highs, at least in terms of the better-quality issues. The lower-quality issues, of course, stayed down. Corrections of this magnitude really are no different than stock market corrections.

It is important to distinguish the LTV bankruptcy from other bankruptcies—for example, the McLean bankruptcy—in looking at the high-income market. There was no broad market reaction to the McLean bankruptcy. McLean had a very high-risk strategy, and it was not a big surprise to many investors that it failed. In contrast, LTV obviously was a troubled credit, but it appeared that survival was likely. In fact, just before the filing, the dollar was beginning to weaken, the steel industry was beginning to improve, and LTV's recapitalization was proceeding along, albeit at a slow pace. Therefore, LTV's bankruptcy announcement was a big surprise, and it did affect the broad market.

Following the insider trading revelations in November, with the associated link to high-income financing, the Fidelity High-Income Fund again declined almost 2 percent in value. In this case, however, the decline was much faster. In the LTV bankruptcy, the Fidelity High-Income Fund experienced $50 million of redemptions over a three-week period. Following the insider trading announcement, the fund experienced $110 million in redemptions over a three-day period. Nevertheless, the market survived both of these storms and moved to new highs.

A sign of maturity is apparent in the market. Investors have been waiting for the other shoe to drop in the insider trading affair; nevertheless, the market has reached new highs. In addition, subsequent pieces of related news—announcements of an indictment or an arrest, a leak to the *Wall Street Journal*, an innuendo, or the regular Friday afternoon rumors—caused smaller declines in the market.

The increase in the number of pension and institutional investors in the high-yield bond market has reduced risk as well. I see an increasing number of unrelated capital pools—equity funds, insurance companies, savings and loans, and foreigners—beginning to take a big piece of the high-income market. This adds an element of stability, because as market declines occur, buyers will materialize sooner as values get more attractive. In other words, the market risk due to a liquidity problem is much lower than it was several years ago.

THE CONTROVERSIAL NATURE OF HIGH-YIELD BONDS

There are three contributing factors to the controversial nature of this market. First, the high-income area is relatively new, by financial market standards; second, there is a general lack of education about this market; and third, the traditional fixed-income mentality is highly risk averse. The controversy is fueled by banks and insurance companies, investment banks, and other institutions that lost clients to this market. This controversy is largely a media event, stemming from a lack of understanding of the true nature of the high-yield issue. Those who do not take the trouble to learn about the high-income market and choose to classify it as pure fixed income always will find controversy; those who choose to classify high income as equity are likely to find controversy; and those who make an effort to understand the market will find fairly little controversy.

The high-income market represented about 5 percent of the total taxable fixed-income corporate market in 1980. I believe it is now 20 to 25 percent of that market, and therefore is quickly coming of age—again, a factor that will reduce the controversy. Five years ago, all high-income portfolios were similar; there were not that many high-income issues. The market now is much broader—not everyone has to own the same issues. For this reason, I believe there will be increasing dispersion of performance among high-income funds, and good credit research and sound investment judgment will play an increasing role in performance.

There are still unresolved questions regarding the high-yield bond market. For example, should savings and loans be permitted to buy high-income bonds, given that these institutions are backed by a government agency? The resolution of that question, favorable or unfavorable, will be irrelevant to the market, except in the very short term. The positive development is that we are going through the process of defining the market and educating everyone about it. Nevertheless, as long as a controversy exists, high-income bonds will continue to be undervalued and provide superior returns. As in all financial markets, when everyone loves them, it will be time to sell; but we are not at that point yet.

The final issue that I want to address is whether the high-income bonds are suitable for institutional investors. Many of the relevant factors have been discussed. First, these issues afford an opportunity to create above-average returns. Second, they have limited risk, as measured by the volatility of returns. Third, liquidity is meaningful now—a dramatic improvement compared to two years ago. In fact, a number of major Wall Street firms are committing resources to secondary trading and research, and are putting up their own capital to participate in the junk bond market. There is now an increasing number of analysts on the buy side, whereas five years ago no buy-side people had high-income bond analysts. Fourth, the suitability of high-income bonds is enhanced by the number of large household names coming to market in the high-yield universe, including Colt Industries, Union Carbide, Phillips Petroleum, FMC, and National Gypsum. Finally, market declines, such as those caused by the LTV bankruptcy and the insider trading scandal are frightening, but no more dangerous than a 100-point crack in the Dow Jones Industrial Average. Although individual high-income bonds are not for the risk averse, I believe that a well-researched, diversified portfolio will come to be viewed as a clear alternative to both stocks and high-grade bonds in a well-balanced institutional investment portfolio.

Question and Answer Session

QUESTION: How can credit be sick if, as Brian Wruble notes, there are so many benefits to leveraged buyouts?

GRANT: I think that the paradox is: If credit is sick, why is the cost of credit on the downslide? Why are interest rates going down? Why are risk premia down? You have to be either very brave or very much the egomaniac to contend that you know more than the market. But I observe that in the face of this roaring bull market in junk, records are being set for credit deterioration. You can see it on all fronts. I do not doubt that people will own securities and people will repackage them. That is a bull market. But investors are not discounting the second coming. The bull market will end.

QUESTION: If equities outperform bonds over reasonable time spans, why bother with equity-like high-yield bonds?

PIKE: Statistics show that there is less volatility in high-yield bonds. I do not know the definition of a reasonable time period, but if the six-year period 1981 to 1986—which included both bear and bull markets in both equity and fixed income—is reasonable, bonds outperformed stocks during that period. In any given year, a roaring bull market in equities probably stands a good chance of outperforming a bull market in bonds, but over a reasonable period of time, I believe these statistics show the opposite.

QUESTION: How do you evaluate the risk associated with companies that enter bankruptcy, even though their balance sheet shows that they can survive?

PIKE: That risk is increasing dramatically. Bankruptcy laws often make it in the interests of management to do a preemptive bankruptcy, even if the company still has liquidity, such as LTV. The LTV filing is a long form, with blanks saying "to be filled in later." This suggests that they did not intend to go bankrupt at that time, but some event triggered them to do it sooner rather than later. Certainly they had adequate liquidity at that moment. For that reason it is important for an analyst to examine the circumstances that might cause a company to protect assets for the shareholders through bankruptcy in addition to performing traditional fixed charges and liquidity analysis.

QUESTION: Please comment on the current LDC debt crisis. Do you think forced lending is the best solution? If not, what else do you suggest?

GRANT: The LDC debt crisis is very interesting. The yields on LDC debt are much lower than what one would expect in the regular high-yield market for those risks. Some of these credits, which have virtually promised that they are not going to pay, are yielding no more than 12 percent. I think forced lending is as wrong a metaphor as the metaphor 'printing money.' In this economy, credit creation is a voluntary act between and among consenting adults. You cannot print money. The Federal Reserve can create bank reserves and invite people to use them. They cannot force the lending. By the same token the banking authorities cannot actually force the lending unless it is by writ, or decree. I think we are going to see a withdrawal of credit from parts of the world which need it most, which is one of the hallmarks of debt contraction. So this is not a bullish argument for the world economy.

QUESTION: Why do high-yield bond buyers tolerate call provisions that allow very little appreciation while the downside risk is almost unlimited?

PIKE: First of all, supply and demand in the marketplace dictate the terms. When there is a shortage of acceptable credits, issues do not have good call protection. When the market is the opposite, there is very good call protection. But there is another reason. A basic underlying philosophy of investing in high-income bonds is that there are going to be a few bankruptcies. Theoretically, the compounding of high income on the 99 issues that work out will more than offset the big decline in the one that goes down. So it is not so much that we are looking for the upside; when we get it, it is a virtue. Nor are we looking for the downside, but occasionally we get caught in it.

QUESTION: What will happen to the high-yield market if Drexel goes out of business?

PIKE: It will fluctuate. In the short run, there probably will be a market panic. In the long run, there will be no effect. Two or three years ago, such an event would have been very serious, but a number of major Wall Street firms have now entered the market in a big way. I believe there are a number of investment bankers who would jump at the opportunity to obtain new business and new clients. It will take a while to digest all of that from the banking point of view, but from the market liquidity point of view, I think firms are retaining substantial liquidity in anticipation of such an eventuality.

GRANT: I agree. I used to think that the market would have a very tough time if Drexel were put out of commission. I do not think that is the case anymore.

QUESTION: Did the Mintz study demonstrate superior returns and relatively low volatility in the early stages of the 1920s, similar to the pattern described by Mr. Pike over the past six years?

GRANT: I am not sure if anyone did any work on volatility at that time, but it would have been a very serene market: it would not have been a volatile market. In terms of return, in the early 1920s government yields were below 5 or 6 percent and trending down, so high-yield securities offered a substantial yield pickup. I think it is instructive also that the establishment came to latch onto this as not only a vehicle for superior returns, but also for social benefits. One of the arguments for high-yield securities—and it is my least favorite—is that they are good for the American worker, and for the American underdog. Drexel, perhaps admitting that it is in greater trouble than we even imagined, has taken to advertising that it is in fact almost an eleemosynary institution because it is providing jobs. Dwight Morrow, the Morgan banker, aristocrat, and ambassador to Mexico, wrote what was almost a prose hymn to the then high-yield market in the pages of *Foreign Affairs* in the late 1920s.[1] He talked almost rhapsodically about the division of international labor and capital, and how the only thing that bound the New York investor or the Japanese borrower was trust. It really was a pretty piece of writing, and that was two years before the break. Which is not to say that history is going to replay like a newsreel, because it never does; but I think that one of the signs of our reaching the more mature—or manic—phases of our own credit boom is that the establishment has had recourse to this idea of the social utility of this market. It is not enough that it goes up; it is also good for us. I am very skeptical of that proposition.

QUESTION: What is an appropriate loan loss reserve for insurance companies and savings and loans holding high-yield debt?

PIKE: It is important to look at the historical default rates in a recession to determine the appropriate reserve level. Look at the worst year, and determine how much loan loss reserves should be. Interestingly, defaults seem to peak the year after a recession, not during the recession itself.

QUESTION: Should Texaco bonds be classified as high-yield or junk bonds, given that management has indicated its intention to file for bankruptcy if it loses the court battle with Penzoil?

PIKE: I would classify them as junk bonds. I do not like to take all-or-none risks. I do not consider myself capable of making a legal judgment as is called for by that situation. But the fact that a company threatens bankruptcy, per se, does not bother me. Any time a company is near restructuring, they are going to put their worst foot forward to try to induce everyone to accept a restructuring that is most favorable to management.

QUESTION: What is an attractive yield spread for high-yield credits, and what do you see happening to spreads in the months ahead?

PIKE: Historically, when the spread between high-yield bonds and long-term government bonds reaches 500 basis points, the market

---

[1]Morrow, Dwight. "Who Buys Foreign Bonds?" *Foreign Affairs* 5, no. 2 (1927): 219–232

becomes very attractive. When it shrinks to 300 basis points, it typically is less attractive, and often cycles back. It is not necessarily a logical cycle. The industry may spend a substantial amount of time at that 300 basis point spread, and even narrow to 280 or 250 basis points; therefore, to get out just as the spread narrows to 300 basis points could be very painful. Conversely, when the spread gets to 500 basis points, it could spend a long time there. With a little more education, experience, and diversity in the market, and the absence of a very severe recession or other bad experience, the spread could possibly narrow to 275 or even 250 basis points before it became unsustainable. What do I see for the spread in the ensuing months? If another shoe does drop, I would say the spreads could widen for a little while. Beyond that, I do not like to make predictions. I believe that we should take a bottoms-up approach, which is: pick an underlying credit that you like and, hopefully, in a bear market it will go down less than the market, and in a bull market it will go up more than the market. Research makes a difference in distinguishing the better credits from the poorer credits. Trying to outguess markets or spreads is a fool's game, especially in the high-income market, which does not have the liquidity of the government markets. In the government market, if the market is going down, you step out one day, and can step back in the next. In the high-income market you cannot do that. Even if you call the top accurately and get out of the market, you may not be able to get back in the market when you want to if you have more than a few million dollars. Buy good credits, and in the long run you will outperform.

The Real Advantages of Synthetic Securities—Part I

Michael R. Asay

Asset-backed securities are undergoing the most rapid change of any fixed-income securities today. Two primary forms of development can be identified. The first is securitization of assets other than mortgages: automobile loans, credit card receivables, boat loans, computer leases, and so forth, which are packaged and sold to investors. The second area is the unbundling and rebundling of cash flows that arise from mortgage instruments, loosely described as synthetic securities.

The motivation for bundling and unbundling is the inherent unpredictability of the cash flows from the traditional fixed-rate residential mortgage. Taking them apart and rebundling them leads to more predictable properties, or at least concentrates the risk in specific pieces that are more readily understood. There are two major developments involved in this repackaging: collateralized mortgage obligations (CMOs) and mortgage-backed security strips (strips). I will focus my discussion on strips.

REVIEW OF STRIP TRANSACTIONS

The first strip transactions were executed in July 1986. There were no strip transactions before that—not because the technology was not available, but because of the tax uncertainty. With a recent Treasury ruling it became clear that strips could be treated as pass-through securities. Fannie Mae (Federal National Mortgage Association) jumped into the market immediately. Since then, the rate of introduction of strips has progressed to somewhere between $500 million and $1 billion a week.

Table 1 lists some of the early strip transactions. These are not complete interest-only (IO) and principal-only (PO) transactions. Instead, two other types of strips are represented. These early transactions took a current coupon security—a 9 percent Fannie Mae, for example—and broke it into a discount class, perhaps a 6 percent coupon, and a premium class, such as a

12 percent coupon (see the B1s and B2s, Table 1). The procedure was to take 50 percent of the principal and allocate it to the discount class, and allocate the remaining 50 percent to the premium class. Then, 3 percentage points of the interest off the 9 was given to the discount class, with the remaining 6 percent going to the premium class. The 3 percent interest divided by $50 worth of principal gives a 6 percent coupon; 6 percent interest divided by $50 principal gives a 12 percent coupon.

This particular type of strip was of interest because it created a discount security with the prepayment profile of a higher coupon security, and a premium security backed by a lower coupon mortgage, which has a lower and more stable prepayment rate. These two new types of securities, which did not exist and could not be created in the market, quickly found niches. The discount 6s were popular with those who were bullish on the market. The lower coupon, with discount price and potential for rapid increase in prepayment rates, was very attractive to those who thought the market was going to rally. It was the longest-duration asset available in the mortgage market.

Likewise, the 12 was a bearish instrument, with more stable prepayment rates than a 12 percent coupon backed by 12s might have had. It found its home in risk-controlled arbitrages with thrifts, and with those who were looking for high-yielding assets but were afraid of the existing high-coupon securities. From the list of transactions in Table 1, it can be seen that most of the examples use this 50/50 form—creating 6s and 12s, or 6.5s and 11.5s from a current coupon mortgage.

In the second form of these early securities, interest was stripped off of a high coupon mortgage which was then sold by itself, leaving a second class with essentially all the principal and a small amount of coupon which was sold as a deep-discount security. The interest-only strip had a nominal amount of principal, so that

Table 1. Summary of FNMA Stripped Mortgage-Backed Securities to Date

Class	Pass-Through Coupon	Weighted Average Coupon	Weighted Average Maturity	Issue Date	Offering Date	Underlying Pool #
A-1	5	11 ½	278	8/86	7/8/86	GL-006893
A-2	605	11 ½	278	8/86	7/8/86	GL-006893
B-1	6	9 ½	265	8/86	7/8/86	GG-006894
B-2	12	9 ½	265	8/86	7/8/86	GG-006894
C-1	6	9 ½	265	8/86	7/21/86	GG-007241
C-2	12	9 ½	265	8/86	7/21/86	GG-007241
D-1	6	9	260	9/86	8/13/86	GG-008240
D-2	11	9	260	9/86	8/13/86	GG-008240
E-1	6	11 ½	281	10/86	9/12/86	GG-008246
E-2	506	11 ½	281	10/86	9/12/86	GG-008246
F-1	6.5	9 ½	264	11/86	10/23/86	GG-008196
F-2	11.5	9 ½	264	11/86	10/23/86	GG-008196
G-1	6.5	9 ½	263	11/86	10/23/86	GG-008197
G-2	11.5	9 ½	263	11/86	10/23/86	GG-008197
H-1	6.5	9 ½	264	11/86	10/23/86	GG-008198
H-2	11.5	9 ½	264	11/86	10/23/86	GG-008198
I-1	6.5	9 ½	262	11/86	10/23/86	GG-008247
I-2	11.5	9 ½	262	11/86	10/23/86	GG-008247
J-1	7	11 ½	283	12/86	11/6/86	GG-035454
J-2	407	11 ½	283	12/86	11/6/86	GL-035454
K-1	6	9	236	12/86	11/6/86	GL-035453
K-2	256	9	236	12/86	11/6/86	GL-035453
L-1	305	8 ½	222	1/87	12/17/86	GL-035471

Total: Classes A, B, C, D, E $200 MM each for a total of $1 billion
Classes F, G, H, I = $700 MM total
Class J = $400 MM
Class K = $300 MM
Class L = $500 MM
IO/PO = $750 MM
Source Goldman, Sachs & Co.

it could be quoted in a traditional way—price per dollar of principal. Because the principal amount was small, however, both the coupon and the price were very high (see Table 1). Because the interest came from a high-coupon mortgage with rapid prepayment rates, the prospects for a prepayment slowdown and enhanced yield were large. This slowdown in rates imparted good hedging qualities to this security.

January 1987 saw the introduction of strips in the logical extreme. In these securities, all the interest off of a mortgage-backed security is assigned to one class (IO), and all of the principal is assigned to another class (PO), as illustrated in Figure 1 using FNMA 9s. The interest-only class is traded on a so-called 'notional' basis. That is if you buy an IO in the market today, you get 9 percentage points of interest, quoted on $100 worth of notional principal.

The beauty of IOs and POs is the ability to create a security with any coupon and prepayment characteristic desired. Again using FNMA

9s, Table 2 illustrates how synthetic coupon securities are created. The simplest security is formed by taking one unit of principal and adding various proportions of interest to it. A 1 percent coupon off Fannie Mae 9s is created by adding .111 units of IO to one unit of PO. The price of the synthetic security would then be the sum of the prices of the principal and the interest, where the latter would be .111 multiplied by its price. An analogous process is followed to create other coupons.

There is a second and cheaper way to create the various coupons, and that is to begin with the underlying Fannie Mae instrument itself, and then add either IO or PO to it. Adding interest to a Fannie Mae increases the coupon. This process is illustrated in Table 3. If you want to create a 12 off of a 9, add 3 percentage points of an IO to a FNMA 9. (Three percentage points of interest would be one-third of a $1mm IO). The synthetic price would be 117–13, derived by adding the two pieces together. Since the cou-

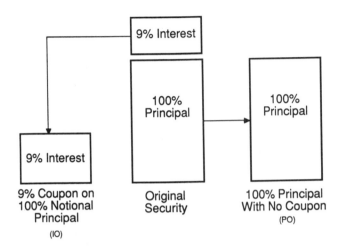

FIGURE 2. Mortgage cash flows at PSA 150 percent

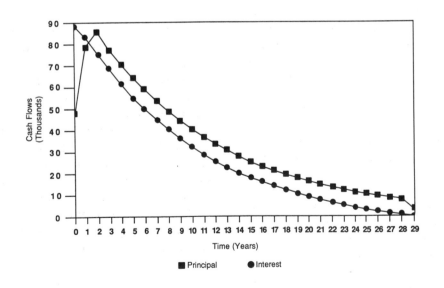

1 MM FNMA 9 percent
Weighted average maturity: 353
Weighted average coupon: 9.85 percent

Source: Goldman, Sachs & Co.

TABLE 2. Synthetic Strip Creation

	Quantity			
Coupon	P/O	I/O	Price	Yield
0	1	0	57–00	7.85
1	1	.111	62.09	7.91
2	1	.222	67–18	7.96
3	1	.333	72–27	8.01
4	1	.444	78–04	8.05
5	1	.555	83–12	8.09
6	1	.666	88–21	8.12
7	1	.777	93–30	8.15
8	1	.888	99–07	8.18
9	1	1.000	104–16	8.21
10	1	1.111	115–02	8.23
11	1	1.222	115–02	8.25
12	1	1.333	120–20	8.27
13	1	1.444	125–20	8.29

Source: Goldman, Sachs & Co.

pon has been increased, this is a more bearish instrument than the original Fannie Mae 9.

Conversely, if one thought the market was going to rally and wanted to decrease the coupon, the opposite technique would be used—again, starting with FNMA 9s, and adding PO to it. For example, to make a 6 off of a 9, add one-half of a unit of PO to the 9, making one-and-a-half units of 6s. The process is illustrated in Table 3. This is a cheaper and easier way of creating strip securities than building them up directly out of the IOs and POs themselves, because of transaction costs.

ECONOMIC PROPERTIES OF STRIPS

The principal and interest cash flows that occur on an underlying mortgage instrument are conditional on the prepayment rate assumption. Figure 2 illustrates the mortgage cash flows for a payment rate of 150 percent PSA, and a 9 percent FNMA. If the prepayment rates on the mortgages change (and prepayment rates are tied to the interest-rate movements) then the cash flows that accrue to the interest-only piece will change. For example, looking at Figure 3, if the prepayment rates are increased, the cash flow that accrues to the IO piece is reduced, because the length of time over which the coupon will be received declines. Conversely, as prepayment rates decrease, the cash flows on the IO increase, as more coupon is received over a longer period.

Figure 4 illustrates the relationship between cash flows on the PO and prepayment rates. In this case, it is the timing, not the volume of the cash, that changes. It is worth remembering that the area underneath the curves is equal to 100 percent of the principal; only the timing of when one gets the principal back changes, but it is important. The faster the prepayment rates, the earlier the return of principal; the slower the prepayment rates, the later the return of principal.

Figure 5 illustrates the price/yield relationship between the IO, the PO, and the underlying mortgage. As the figure indicates, when interest rates rise, the value of the IO will increase, because the length of time over which cash flows on the IO are received is extended. The investor is getting more total coupon. In contrast, the PO looks more like a traditional bond; when rates fall, the price goes up. The price change with respect to interest rates is asymmetric, however. When rates fall, accelerating prepayment rates force the PO price up

TABLE 3. Synthetic Strips off FNMA 9s

To *increase* Coupon: ADD I/O
  Example: 12s - add 3% or ⅓ unit I/O to 9s
       Price = 102–02 + 15–11 = 17–13

To *decrease* Coupon: ADD P/O
  Example: 6s off 9s: Add ½ unit P/O to 9s
       Price = 102–02 + 26–0 = 128–02
       128–02/1.5 = 85.38 = per million

Source: Goldman, Sachs & Co.

FIGURE 3. Interest-only cash flows

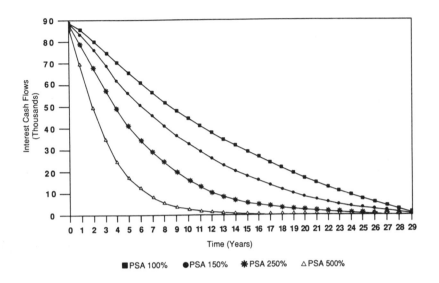

FIGURE 4. Principal-only cash flows

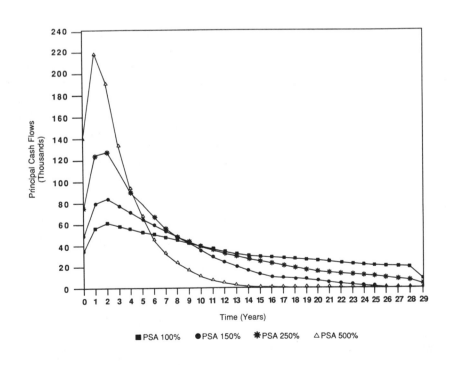

Source: Goldman, Sachs & Co.

FIGURE 5. FNMA prinicipal-only/interest-only stripped mortgage-backed securities

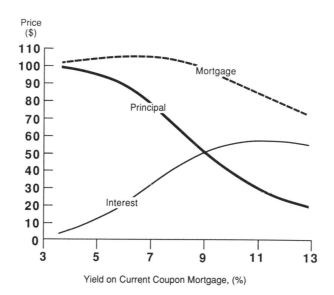

Yield on Current Coupon Mortgage, (%)

Principal and interest from FNMA 9 percent
Weighted average maturity: 353
Weighted average coupon: 9.85 percent

Source: Goldman, Sachs & Co.

rapidly. On the other side, an increase in rates will slow prepayments only modestly, and the price falls less. Looking at the shapes of the strip curves, IOs and POs move directly in opposition to one another. IOs move directly with interest rates, and have so-called negative duration. POs have a much steeper price curve than the mortgages themselves, and behave more like a standard bond.

The properties of strips are very dependent upon the particular mortgage on which they are based. Clearly, all IOs and POs are critically dependent on the prepayment rates inasmuch as they were created to isolate the different prepayment features. Figure 6 shows prepayment assumptions for alternative coupon mortgage-backed strips in different interest-rate environments. Figure 7 illustrates the IO price profiles for the different coupon securities with these prepayment assumptions. The slope of the pricing functions at the zero interest rate change point (on the horizontal axis) is interesting. Starting with the Fannie Mae 11s, the price

on the IO is very low, as expected, because the prepayment rates are very fast, and the present value of expected cash flows is low. When interest rates rise and the prepayment rates slow down dramatically, however, the value of that IO increases rapidly. This IO has limited downside and substantial upside potential. The 9s, which are prepaying slowly, have a high price. If interest rates rise, prepayment rates are not going to slow down dramatically. Consequently, the price appreciation potential on the 9 IOs is less than on the 11s. The 9s, however, have more downside risk, because prepayments may accelerate rapidly.

This analysis may be put into an options context. For example, the Fannie Mae 11 IOs closely resemble a long position in a put. If interest rates rise, the value increases dramatically. In the same way, a Fannie Mae 9 IO is similar to being short in a call, with limited upside potential and a great deal of downside risk.

Figure 8 illustrates the shape of the PO strips. At the zero rate change point, the price of

FIGURE 6.   Prepayment assumptions

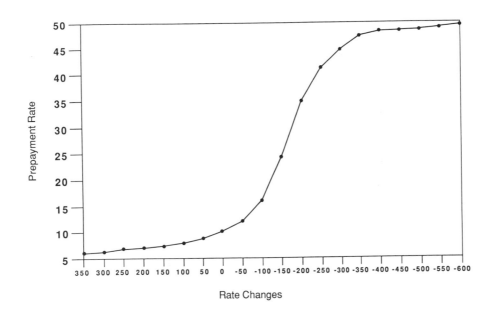

FIGURE 7.   FNMA Interest-only strips—scenario price changes

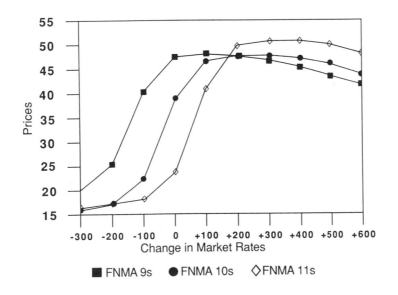

Source: Goldman, Sachs & Co.

FIGURE 8.   FNMA Principal-only strips—scenario price changes

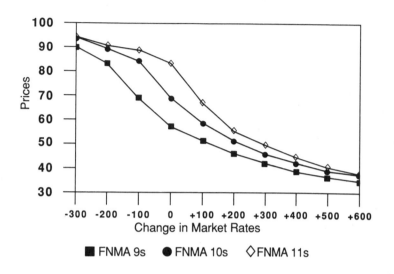

Source: Goldman, Sachs & Co.

the Fannie Mae 11 POs are high, because the prepayment rates are rapid and the cash flow is occurring early. As rates rise and the prepayment rates slow, the value of the PO declines, because the timing of the cash flow is pushed into the future. The downside potential on the 11s is substantial, because prepayment rates can only slow from their high level.

The upside potential is limited because the instrument already has a short duration.

The 9 POs, on the other hand, have good upside potential if the market rallies. The prepayment rates on the underlying collateral may accelerate rapidly, and that will translate into rapid price appreciation. When rates rise, however, prepayments will not fall substantially, and so the price does not fall dramatically. Translating these again into an options position,

the 11s resemble a short position in a put; the 9s are more like a call.

Together, the IOs and POs cover the spectrum with regard to the various types of option positions, and any option combination is therefore possible. A straddle, for example, could be created by purchasing an IO off 11s and a PO off 9s. Of course, the pricing profiles of different strips translate into different yields in the stable rate environments. Long option positions have low yield, while short option positions have high yield.

Strips open the door to a large number of new, efficient trading and hedging strategies. As they become better understood, the market will grow, and strips will be included as part of every efficient mortgage portfolio.

The Real Advantage of Synthetic Securities—Part II

Michael D. Youngblood

A synthetic mortgage instrument is a security that manipulates the constituent cash flows of a pool of mortgage loans or mortgage pass-through securities. In a synthetic instrument, principal and interest components are separated from the combined cash flow stream. The separation of principal and interest into strips has been examined intensively; so has the collateralized mortgage obligation (CMO) and its derivative structures. The most powerful of these derivative structures is CMO equity, or the residual cash flows.

CMO equity truly is the most complex and powerful of mortgage instruments in existence today. It deserves attention because it is a paradigm of the return profiles available from all mortgage instruments. In one form of CMO equity, the bearish pattern of returns identical to the interest-only (IO) strip can be found. In another form of CMO equity, one can find a bullish pattern of returns, substantially the same as the principal-only (PO) strip. In addition, CMO equity affords a third kind of return pattern: a neutral return pattern that provides exceptionally high yields unless interest rates move to higher or lower extremes from the status quo.

CMO equity has three important characteristics. First, it has impeccable quality. It is, after all, the leftover cash flows from a collateralized mortgage obligation, which until recently was uniformly triple-A rated by both rating agencies. Second, CMO equity offers extremely high yields in today's market environment. The cash-flow yields range from 10 to 15 percent. This is precisely the range of returns that one would expect from a high-yield or so-called junk bond security. In fact, CMO equity and high-yield debt offer comparable yields for the same basic reason: they have a similar standard deviation of returns, which is extraordinarily high across a range of interest-rate environments. CMO equity responds to changes in interest rates; junk bonds respond to changes in corporate credit in different economic environments. Third, CMO equity has a short average life, or effective term.

COLLATERALIZED MORTGAGE OBLIGATIONS

Before discussing the CMO equity in greater detail, let us examine the CMO and the source of residual cash flows. CMOs are multiclass debt securities collateralized by pools of mortgages. These debt securities are retired sequentially. In the classic four-bond type of CMO, the first class or tranche—typically called the A tranche—receives all payments until it is retired, and then the second, or B tranche, receives all payments until it is retired, and so on until the end of the CMO. The last tranche usually is called the Z tranche. It is possible to structure a CMO so that some of the tranches receive simultaneous payments. They may also be designed to carry fixed or floating rates of interest.

CMOs create a sequential or simultaneous band of payment classes with different effective lives, or weighted average lives. Part of the reason for their existence is related to the arbitrage potential built into the CMO market itself. Fundamentally, the issuer is exploiting the difference in the cash flow yield of a pool of mortgage collateral and the weighted average cost of a series of bonds. In today's yield curve environment, the shortest bond—the class A or tranche A—will have the lowest cost of debt. In today's market, this tranche is priced at 90 basis points over the two- or three-year Treasury rate. In contrast, the class Z, or Z bond, which often is an accrual bond, is priced at about 150 basis points over the yield on 20–year Treasury bonds. It is possible to price each of the tranches to yield competitive market rates and still have some principal and interest payments left over.

CMO EQUITY

CMO equity is the residual in the CMO trust after satisfaction of the debt obligations. Cash flows come in monthly through the bond trustee, and are distributed quarterly or semiannually to the bondholders. In the interim period, the cash flows are reinvested. The excess is distributed contemporaneously to the equity holders.

The primary source of CMO equity is the arbitrage difference between the yield on the pool of mortgage collaterals and the cost of the series of bonds issued to fund them. This will work differently with a fixed-rate versus a floating-rate CMO. In a fixed-rate CMO, this arbitrage potential or spread between a yield and a cost is concentrated in the shortest tranche—the A tranche—because it will have the lowest cost of debt. The B tranche, which typically is priced off the five-year yield, will narrow the spread to a very small amount. The C and D tranches usually will provide for either no spread at all, or just enough to carry on the operational and administrative expenses of the CMO trust.

Therefore, the life of the A tranche is critical to the returns of the equity holder. The longer the A tranche survives in an environment of high interest rates and low prepayment rates, the greater the flow of income to the equity holder. Conversely, in an environment of falling interest rates and accelerating prepayment rates, the A tranche will melt away, leaving very little income to be earned and distributed to the equity holders. Therefore, it has a pattern of returns essentially the same as the IO strip.

A floating-rate CMO produces more complex cash-flow patterns. With a floating-rate CMO, the movement of the London Interbank Offered Rate (LIBOR) governs the yield of the floating-rate tranche, because these presently are priced between 35 and 60 basis points over one-month, three-month, or six-month LIBOR. If interest rates rise, the LIBOR-based rate will increase to the cap imposed on the floating-rate tranche, reducing the arbitrage spread. In a market rally, the LIBOR rate will fall, magnifying the spread available to the equity holders.

The cash-flow pattern is complicated by the variance of prepayments on the underlying mortgage securities. While LIBOR will increase in a rising interest-rate environment, prepayments will slow. In fact, the prepayments dom-inate the increase in LIBOR for the first 100 or 200 basis points of an upward interest-rate move, allowing the high initial yields to the equity holders to remain unchanged. On the other hand, in a market rally, the effect of the falling LIBOR will dominate accelerating prepayment rates for the first 100 to 200 basis points of the rally. Thereafter, the effect of rapid prepayment rates will melt away the A tranche and leave very little income to the equity holder, even though the yield spread is widened, leading to a neutral pattern of returns. As long as there is low volatility and a stable pattern of interest-rate movements, within positive or negative 200 basis points, double-digit cash-flow yields are possible. Beyond those bounds, one ends up with a 3 to 5 percent diminished return.

Reinvestment income is another source of return to the equity holder. Mortgages pay monthly, but they are held for quarterly or semiannual distribution by the CMO structure itself; thus, the equity holder benefits from reinvestment of these funds. Also, for various reasons, a bond reserve fund may be created in a CMO, particularly a CMO that utilizes whole mortgage loan collateral. Income earned on the reserve fund accrues to the equity holder, and this can be significant—I have seen a $500 million CMO with a $7 million bond reserve fund.

Perhaps the most interesting source of return to equity holders is the principal differential. From time to time, due to various tax considerations, one is obliged to overcollateralize the CMO. The case of the Salomon Brothers CMO Trust 13 is illuminating. It was a monthly-pay CMO based on 9 percent, 15-year Freddie Mac (Federal Home Loan Mortgage Corporation) mortgage securities. These securities were selling at a significant discount, with a yield of 12 percent. In an environment of accelerating prepayment rates, an equity holder recovers that discount over a shorter time horizon, driving returns higher. Conversely, slower prepayment rates will extend the period of the recovery of the discount and diminish yields. This is exactly what happens with principal-only strips.

Therefore, CMO equity, depending on the structure of the CMO and the type of collateral contributed to it, can duplicate all of the return patterns that have been examined thus far, in addition to the uniquely neutral return pattern found in floating-rate CMOs. The Salomon Brothers Trust 2–4 is a good example. This trust is fundamentally dependent on the life of the A tranche. One starts with a 10.80 percent cash flow yield, and if the market drops 300 basis points, returns can skyrocket to 20 percent. Unfortunately, one gets the reverse side in a rally, with returns of minus 14 percent.

CMO equity has a relatively short average life, which distinguishes it from interest-only (IO) and principal-only (PO) strips. CMO equity will survive only over the life of the A tranche, which is its primary source of returns. The average life of a CMO is three to six years, with a duration of three years and recovery of capital in five years. Approximately 22 percent of the investment outlay is recovered annually in gross cash flows to the equity holders; so $22 of every $100 of the investment will come back each year, ending the investment in roughly a five-year period. This is a lavish cash flow, short-term instrument.

CONCLUSION

In summary, the key virtues of an equity CMO are the high credit quality built into the instrument itself; the high cash-flow yields, with the promise of higher yields in an appropriate interest rate environment; and the very short life. The trade-off is a vulnerability to changes in LIBOR and prepayment rates that lead to a high standard deviation of returns across different interest-rate and economic environments.

Linked-Debt Instruments in Institutional Portfolios—Part I

Joel W. Miller

Innovation means new ways of doing things, but asset-linked securities are very old; gold-backed dollars and other gold-backed currencies have existed for years. Gold-backed railroad bonds existed until the 1930s. The interesting thing about asset-linked securities today is that most of the securities are being issued as a way to control volatility or risk; previously, gold-backed securities were probably a response to credit concerns.

Since the period of high interest rates and increased volatility in the early 1980s, issuers have become more aggressive in seeking ways of controlling risk and reducing debt service costs. Indeed, virtually any structure that provides a lower net issuance cost will receive serious consideration from issuers. As a result, markets have moved from bonds indexed to traditional assets, such as gold and oil, to bonds linked to currencies, stock market indexes, and rates of inflation. The prevailing attitude seems to be, "If it fluctuates, securitize it." Even the best ideas will not lead to a security that gains a significant market share, however, unless it serves an investor need.

Asset-linked securities serve several needs. First, they allow investors to purchase long-dated options that do not exist on regulated exchanges. The result is a vehicle for controlling risk over longer periods than are possible on exchanges, because most exchange contracts only go out two years, and the liquidity on longer contracts is rather poor.

Second, and more important, an institution that cannot hold a physical asset, or is restricted from trading futures, may purchase an equivalent indexed security which provides the same risk/reward profile or allows the hedging of risks taken elsewhere in the portfolio. Investors also may create synthetic securities using OTC (over-the-counter) traded asset-linked bonds and exchange-traded futures.

Potential regulation is an important issue. Asset-linked securities may come under some form of regulation by the Commodities Futures Trading Commission (CFTC) instead of the Securities and Exchange Commission (SEC), because commodities are supposed to be regulated by the CFTC. The CFTC must decide what they will permit. For example, because many of the new asset-linked securities have been traded in the Euromarket where the CFTC has no jurisdiction, a ruling favoring exchange-based trading could serve to exclude U.S.-based investors and issuers from the U.S. domestic market for these securities.

There are two arguments against exchange-based trading of asset-linked securities: poor liquidity for long-dated contracts, and lack of uniformity. The lack of uniformity actually is one of the biggest advantages of the asset-linked market, because it permits the creation of a security that does absolutely anything. The absence of conventional futures contracts in the five- to ten-year areas is also an argument against exchange-based trading. The ability to negotiate tailored terms to the specific market is a big advantage for people who want to hedge longer-term risks because of the poor liquidity in other markets.

The OTC asset-linked and exchange-traded commodities markets complement each other. The option components of two- to seven-year asset-linked securities may be hedged by rolling the nearby exchange-traded future forward.

Market-related risks may not be the biggest pitfall in investing in linked securities from a portfolio perspective. Tax and legal issues must also be considered. Tax considerations may have a much greater impact on potential returns. If a security is issued in the domicile of the issuer, it usually is subject to withholding taxes to foreigners at a treaty rate ranging from zero percent to 30 percent, although the treaty would exclude supranational issuers. Paying taxes may also reduce the returns to investors below those of alternative investments. If an institution is tax exempt, however, it usually can get an exemption from withholding. For a taxable investor, the withholding problem may be solved by dealing in the Euromarket, because investments in this market generally are not subject to withholding taxes.

The Euromarket may not be the best solution for all investors. Recently there has been an enormous flow of capital between countries. Deregulation and liberalization of tax laws have resulted in lower treaty tax rates, as well as elimination of withholding taxes, in some cases. Since most Eurobond issues also guarantee the holder the stated interest rate, any change in tax laws would result in withholding taxes being paid by the issuer. Most indentures are written with a tax-related extraordinary par call provision at the issuer's option. Consequently, the investor may hedge perfectly and still lose, because there is tax-related event risk that cannot be hedged away.

INVESTMENT CHARACTERISTICS OF ASSET-LINKED SECURITIES

The risk borne by the issuer of an asset-linked security is determined by how the issue is indexed. For example, the security may be structured so that the principal payment is indexed and the interest payments are fixed. Similarly, the security may provide for indexed coupons and a fixed principal payment, or a bond may provide for an indexing of both principal and interest. Alternatively, interest payments may be fixed to one index, such as inflation, and principal payments fixed to another, such as a stock market index. As the market has evolved, securities have been indexed using retail price inflation in the UK, stock market indexes on major exchanges around the world—Paris, New York, Tokyo, and Sydney—raw materials, and individual U.S. Treasury bonds. The structural possibilities are virtually limitless.

An asset-linked security may combine the investment characteristics of a bond with the features of options, futures, or swaps. The option portion may be offered in the form of a detachable warrant, which is more desirable in terms of the risk of a call. The asset conversion ratio may be either fixed at issue, or based on the value of the index at some future date, or constructed as a spread between two assets. The asset may have a floating rate or a fixed rate; it may also have a floor, a ceiling, or a collar around the index. The security is considered a bull security when it moves with the index, and a bear security when it moves against the index. If the issuer combines two sides into a single bull/bear security, all index risks can be passed onto the investors. This type of security may maximize the issuer's goal of reducing all-in cost while shifting as much risk as possible to the holder.

Asset-linked securities are not uniform because each investment bank creates its own formula for indexing as the market moves over time. An issuer may have different strike or exercise prices for the same asset. Tracking the different formulas creates some problems in terms of analysis.

The U.S. market is characterized by a lack of good information. There is no Moody's bond manual on asset-linked securities, and collecting details on individual issues may be quite tedious. In addition, valuation is a problem. There is not an option model available which can properly value the option component on longer maturity issues. In fact, when we valued the oil option component on Sohio, which was going out only 3.5 to 5 years, we checked the values of our model against those of several other models and received a puzzling wide range of values.

The uncertainty of valuing the option component makes it more difficult for dealers and investors to hedge their positions. In fact, several recent Euromarket gold-related bull/bear issues were severely mispriced; this reduced liquidity and damaged the market's confidence to a small degree.

ASSET-LINKED SECURITIES: EXAMPLES

Silver-Indexed Bonds

Sunshine Mining issued silver-indexed bonds in April 1980. The issue was rated B at the time. The company issued $25 million bonds, at 8.5 percent, due April 15, 1995. The issue is noteworthy for two reasons. First, it was an example of an early attempt to control risk. The issue really is the equivalent of a convertible bond with silver substituted for equity. Sunshine sold debt indexed to 50 ounces of silver for a gain of between 400 and 450 basis points versus the B-rated market and suffered no equity dilution.

The bonds were a lien on the production of silver, at a time when Sunshine was the third largest silver producer in the United States. Only the principal was indexed.

The second reason the Sunshine issue is noteworthy is that it underscores the importance of analyzing the underlying credit risk rather than simply buying an option on an asset. With the subsequent plunge in silver prices—from $50 an ounce in 1980 to approximately $6 an ounce in 1983—the company's mines were no longer economical to operate, and mining was suspended in 1986. The silver-indexed bonds were exchanged for new issues which pay the coupon in stock of Sunshine Mining. If the price of silver does not recover, this is not a good investment, even if fully hedged.

The "Giscard"

The second issue of interest is the "Giscard" or French government 15-year bond issue issued July 16, 1973 and due in 1988. It is triple-A rated, backed by the French government, and was originally sold for 5.5 billion French francs. At that time, the French franc was gold-backed. As a backstop to France going off the gold standard, the issue was tied to the December 1972 kilo price of an ingot of gold on the Paris Bourse, which was 10,480 French francs, equivalent to about $30 an ounce. One of the interesting things about this bond is that both the coupon and the principal were indexed to gold, with the result that the yield to maturity is always 7 percent as long as the price of gold does not change. If the price of gold declines, however, one collects the coupon payments and gets the original investment back. If, on the other hand, the price of gold rises, one collects more than the 7 percent coupon payments in the interim. The coupon payments were initially subject to a 10 percent withholding tax, but that was eliminated in December 1985. The principal payment is free from withholding.

The issue appears to have currency risk, but in fact, because the Giscard is indexed to gold, which is priced in U.S. dollars, there is no currency risk. Initially, people were concerned about how they could hedge the French franc. Once they realized that there was no currency risk, the amount of trading in the bond became enormous. In early 1985, French government bonds yielded 10 percent for three-year maturities. A fully hedged position in this indexed issue, using exchange-traded futures, yielded 21 percent for three years.

On July 16, 1985, the bond investment would have looked as follows: The kilo price of gold was 90,000 French francs, or about $323 per ounce. Dividing 90,000 French francs by 10,480 gives an index ratio of 8.588, so the anticipated French franc flow would have gone from the original 70 francs at issue to 601.16 French francs. At a foreign exchange rate at that time of 8.67 francs per dollar, the dollar coupon flow would be $69.34 on an investment of $999.20. Both the French franc and U.S. dollar internal rates of return would have been 7 percent annually.

By January 1987, the actual results in U.S. dollars yielded a much higher return than anticipated. The internal rate of return on a U.S. dollar basis was over 24 percent, versus less than 1 percent on a French franc basis. With a 26 percent increase in the price of gold, up to 80,400 French francs per kilo or about $405 per ounce, a French franc investor had almost a negative return due to a 10.7 percent decline in the French franc price of the issue from 90,000 to 80,400. Thus, an investor who thought he or she was buying a French franc denominated security was actually taking a great deal of currency risk, and would have been better off in another security.

Oil-Indexed Notes

The third asset-linked issue that I would like to discuss is the Standard Oil Company Oil-Indexed Notes. The Oil Indexed Notes were issued as part of a unit, consisting of a Series A 6.30 percent OID due in 2001, and Series B (1991) and C (1997) zero coupon notes with an option component indexed to oil. This option component operates in the following way: The notes represent 13,875,000 barrels of petroleum; at expiration, the payoff will be stepped up by the amount by which actual oil prices exceed $25 per barrel, with a cap of $40 per barrel.

Given the yields at the time and the market-place for similar zeros coupon bonds, the intrinsic value of the option for the shorter oil-indexed note was only $1.49 a barrel, while the longer oil-indexed note was $1.66 a barrel, both of which in retrospect were probably pretty reasonable. Many investors did not like the fact that the issue was capped at $40 a barrel, but given the total market risk on 13,875,000 barrels of oil that Sohio was assuming, they actually were at risk for future contingent interest payments of $208 million (or 13,875,000 × 15). In retrospect, that may not have been such a good bet, unless one felt that oil prices would be below $25 a barrel when the zeros matured in 1991 and 1997.

Linked-Debt Instruments in Institutional Portfolios—Part II

Rodney L. Gray

The oil industry has recently experienced a great amount of fluctuation as a result of interest-rate volatility, oil and gas prices, and deregulation of the natural gas industry. Under such conditions it is natural for oil and gas firms to consider the issuance of securities indexed on petroleum or other energy prices. To illustrate this possibility, I would like to use as an example an oil/interest-rate security that was presented to Transco Energy Company in 1986.

In my opinion, the treasurer of Transco has three responsibilities. The first responsibility is to minimize the cost of capital. The second is to try to minimize funding risk by making sure that the amount of debt coming due does not put pressure on the internal cash flows. The third responsibility is to maximize financial flexibility. This latter deals mostly with debt covenants and with examining the debt to equity relationship, which is a major consideration in every issue. It is important that the company is not hindered in taking advantage of future investment opportunities.

In 1986, a proposal for an oil-linked security was presented to Transco. The security would have had a five-year maturity and a yield that was 115 basis points over the five-year Treasury rate. The issue was linked to oil; it was nominally convertible into 50 barrels of oil per $1000 bond, with a strike price of $20. A cap of $45 was placed on the value of the oil per barrel. The issue was convertible at any time at the option of the issuer. Thus, the issue effectively gave the investor an ability to put the bond for petroleum priced at between $20 and $45 per share.

In reviewing this product, Transco's management examined the cost of capital, the funding risks, flexibility considerations, forecasts of oil prices and interest rates, and the other alternatives. In terms of cost of capital, this issue was attractive, since it was priced at only 115 basis points over Treasury yields; at the time, Transco was paying 240 basis points over the Treasury rate. According to Transco's forecast, the Treasury rate was at a relatively low point, and the yield would start to increase in the near future. Similarly, the firm's oil price forecast—which generally tracks along with interest rates—indicated that oil prices would be around $16 in the summer, and would increase to $21 in late 1987 or early 1988. Looking at that forecast, the $20 strike price seemed rather low.

As far as financial flexibility, management believed that the put aspect made the financial flexibility and the funding risk considerations go hand in hand. It is desirable to lock in the cost of capital: volatility is not desirable either in the issues one buys nor in the issues one sells. Therefore, in this case the put feature was hard to accept, particularly in terms of the trouble it would cause in analyzing Transco's liability portfolio and its performance in the future. It would require endless sensitivity analyses that seemed too difficult to handle from an issuer's perspective.

Finally, the funding alternatives had to be examined. What other approaches could Transco follow? In management's view, interest rates and Treasury yields were at a relatively low point and would rise; the corporate spread would improve; and oil prices would start to rise. They forecast that the credit spread on an oil company would improve significantly. Therefore, Transco's strategy in 1986 was to put a hedge on the underlying Treasury rate, locked in at around 6.65 percent, for five years.

After deciding not to issue an oil-linked security, management began to think about the conditions under which such a security might be appropriately issued. They have not been able to arrive at an answer. One strategy is to issue the security when interest rates and oil prices are at a peak. That makes sense, as both would tend to go down together following the issue, and therefore would not trigger the strike price. The only problem with that scenario is if interest rates are at a peak, one is locked in at a very high interest rate. Therefore, management concluded that an oil-linked security that is the reverse of the security that was presented would be more attractive—for example, an oil-linked security that includes a high premium, or a higher rate at the time of issuance in exchange for a floating rate that would come down when oil prices decline.

Interest rates and oil prices continue to show great volatility. This volatility has generated many innovations. The oil-linked security that was presented to Transco was very intriguing. It seemed like a way of achieving a low financing cost with a natural hedge. Upon full analysis, however, my conclusion is that other alternatives, such as the conventional fixed-rate instruments, executed at the right time and managed with other financial instruments such as swaps and caps, provide a better alternative to Transco than the oil-linked security.

The Next Decade in the Economy

Jay W. Forrester

There is no widely-accepted theory on why short-term business cycles occur, to say nothing of the major depressions. For example, in the 1970s, there was great puzzlement over so-called stagflation; simultaneously rising inflation and unemployment was considered impossible. I have discovered that nearly all modes of behavior seen in real life are a result of local decision-making processes. A model built on the decision-making processes in the corporate world, in banking, and in the Federal Reserve—the microstructure of the economy—manifests all of the modes of behavior seen in real life. These behaviors include: 1) business cycles, with peaks 3 to 5 years apart; 2) the economic long wave with peaks some 45 to 60 years apart; 3) money inflation, that part of inflation or price change that is attributed to money supply increasing faster than real activity; and 4) long-term growth trends that depend on population growth and changes in technology. I will focus this presentation on the economic long wave. I believe the economic long wave has great significance for the next decade. Nearly all discussions of economics in the business press take place in the context of short-term business cycles. There is, however, something far more important occurring—a longer mode of behavior on top of which the business cycle itself rides.

Before continuing, I should point out that the ideas presented here regarding the economic long wave are not generally accepted in American academic economics. The economic long wave has been largely ignored in theoretical economics in America. It is taken more seriously in Europe.

THE MODEL

The framework I use to examine the behavior of the economy is based on the System Dynamics National Model, which has been developed over the past 10 years. The model itself reflects 20 years of prior work on how the policies of corporations produce their growth, stability, successes, and failures.

The system dynamics modeling process is very different from more familiar econometric models. The model is built up from policies being followed in business units, and shows what happens when those policies and information flows interact with one another. A computer simulation model uses a role-playing procedure that involves setting up a replica of the decision-making processes in an organization. In doing this, one often discovers that well-known policies within an organization cause difficulties. In other words, behavior of a social system is determined internally to a much greater extent than most people believe. The blame for difficulties is usually placed on the outside world, but instead the problems often come from internal structure and policies that determine behavior.

In the early 1970s, my group at the Massachusetts Institute of Technology (MIT) was asked by the Rockefeller Brothers Fund to apply the system dynamics approach to understanding economic behavior. We started with the belief that we could obtain a model of the national economy if we worked upward from the corporate level of decision-making. Using such a model, we could come to a better understanding of the behavior that has been so puzzling in the economic world. This turns out to be true. A system dynamics model built from well-known local business and banking policies exhibits the wide range of economic behavior that has been so confusing in the past.

THE ECONOMIC LONG WAVE

The economic long wave, also known as the Kondratieff cycle, has received little acceptance because there has been no theory on how it could occur. Without a theory to explain behavior, there was a tendency to view the great depressions as special cases or accidents—situations that have occurred because of wars, the discovery of gold, or great inventions.

Now there is a theory of the economic long wave. A computer simulation model is a theory of the behavior that the model produces. The theory embodied in a model involves assumptions about the policies being followed and about the structure of the system. The National Model contains policies governing low-level decisions familiar to operating managers. By using the National Model, one can evaluate policies for pricing goods, borrowing money, setting interest rates, hiring people, and ordering capital plant. One also can compare behavior of the model against real life to explain what is occurring in the actual economy. The National Model provides an important interpretation of history against which to examine current economic events.

It has been said that "those who ignore history must relive it." History teaches us lessons; but what history should we be learning from? Should the present be judged against the history of the 1960s and 1970s—which I believe most people are doing—or should it be judged against the history of some other era?

In my view, the 1920s are the most recent years that are analogous to the present. Similar economic conditions also existed around 1830 and 1890. To make such a statement, one must have a theory or framework that shows why the 1830s, 1890s, 1920s, and 1980s are similar. The economic long wave provides such a framework. We believe that the economic long wave is the behavior mode that has produced the major depressions—the ones that were each called "The Great Depression" during the period in which they occurred. The great depressions are a phenomenon that occurs at intervals of 45 to 60 years, for reasons that are intrinsic to the technology, decision-making, and information flows in the economic structure. The long wave is a consequence of how we conduct our affairs. The long-wave is not inescapable. Given our tendency toward short-run objectives,we do things that lay a foundation for great excesses, and the major depressions follow.

There are many relationships in an economy that feed economic long-wave behavior. I will discuss only three of these relationships as representative of a number of others.

The first relationship is the so-called "bootstrap" or "self-ordering" process within the capital sectors, illustrated in Figure 1. Consider aggregating all of the industries that produce capital plant. Then imagine that the consumer-goods sectors order slightly more capital equipment. The capital-producing businesses would need to increase their output to meet the demand. To increase output, capital producers would themselves need more capital plant. This process is destabilizing. As demand for capital increases, demand for capital in the capital sector goes up, and the capital sector itself orders capital. The increased demand leads to increased backlogs or reductions in inventory, increased growth expectations, and increased demand for capital equipment, all of which produce more ordering by the capital sector.

Self-ordering processes exist in many areas of an economy. I grew up on a Nebraska cattle ranch. In the cattle industry, when more beef is ordered by consumers, prices go up and inventories go down. Higher prices and shortages move back toward the cattle ranches, which then have incentives to increase the output of beef. One increases beef output only by increasing the breeding herds, which is accomplished by withholding female cattle from the market. So the first thing that occurs when you want more beef is that you get less. This is quite contrary to the idea of simple supply/demand curves in economics. The self-ordering process is highly destabilizing. When you want more beef and the price goes up, you get less. Then, the price goes up still more, which for a time encourages people all along the supply line to provide less. That is the fundamental explanation for the 14-year price cycle in cattle. Cattle have a 9-month gestation period, a 2-year age to maturity, and an 8-year effective breeding life, which produces a 14-year price cycle. It should not be surprising that this same process in capital plant, where the gestation period is two or three years and the life is far more than eight years, defines a mode of behavior with a periodicity of some 50 years from peak-to-peak.

Second, real interest rates destabilize production of physical capital. Assuming a constant nominal interest rate, as the demand for capital goes up, the price of capital rises (see Figure 2). As the price of capital rises, the real interest rate on that capital goes down, real interest being the nominal interest rate minus the inflation rate in price of capital plant. As the real interest rate goes down, the demand for capital intensity increases, which raises demand for capital. This feedback loop accentuates the demand for cap-

FIGURE 1. Self-ordering by the capital-producing sector

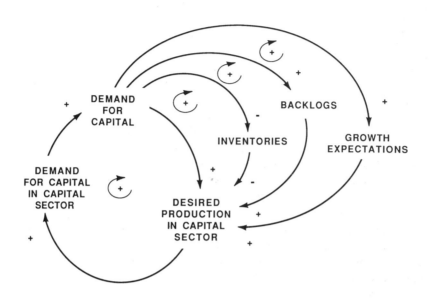

FIGURE 2. Real interest rate destabilizes production of physical capital

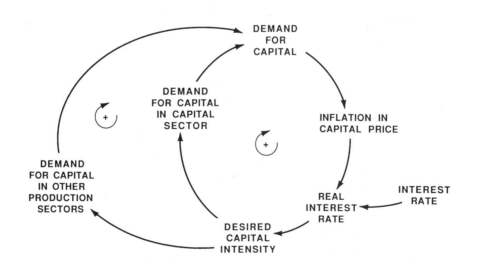

Source: MIT System Dynamics Group

TABLE 1. History of Real Interest Rates

	Period	Average Real Interest Rate
1870–1894	(Downturn)	8.0
1894–1923	(Upturn)	1.6
1923–1938	(Downturn)	4.3
1923–1932	(Interim)	8.0
1938–1979	(Upturn)	−1.1
1950–1979	(Interim)	0.6
1979–1985		9.9

Source: MIT System Dynamics Group

ital plant during an expansion. The reverse occurs during a downturn.

Evaluating a theory calls for examining both the logic of the internal structure of the model and what is occurring in real life. Table 1 shows the history of real interest. In the 1870 to 1894 downturn period, the real interest rate was 8 percent. In the upturn of 1894 to 1923, real interest fell to 1.6 percent. From 1923 to 1938, a downturn period, real interest averaged around 4 percent. On a shorter-term basis, 1923 to 1932, the average real interest rate was 8 percent; in 1931, it was 12 to 14 percent. The current discussion of unprecedentedly high real interest rates is unfounded. In fact, they were higher in the early 1930s. During the upturn period after 1938, the real interest rate was negative—about −1 percent. From 1950 to 1979, it was about 0.6 percent. Most recently, from 1979 to 1984, real interest has been almost 10 percent, as the economy moves into another downturn. In other words, the real interest rate has been fluctuating with the rise and fall of the economic long wave.

The third driving force in the economic long-wave arises from the interaction between real wage shifts and the demand for capital plant. As illustrated in Figure 3, demand in the capital sector increases labor hiring, reduces labor availability, and pushes up real wages. Higher real wages makes capital plant more attractive. Cost of labor shifts relative to cost of capital in a manner that increases the demand for capital plant during an upturn and reduces demand for capital during a downturn. Table 2 shows the history of growth in real wage. From

FIGURE 3. Real wage shifts the demand for capital plant

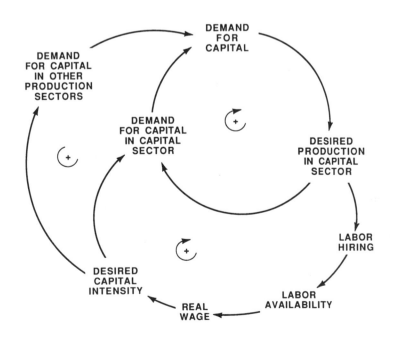

Source: MIT System Dynamics Group

TABLE 2. History of Growth in Real Wage in the U.S.

Period	Growth Rate (% Per Year)
1870–1894 (Downturn)	0.95
1894–1923 (Upturn)	2.01
1923–1938 (Downturn)	0.97
1938–1973 (Upturn)	2.76
1979–1985	0.04

Source: MIT System Dynamics Group

1870 to 1894, a downturn period, the growth rate in real wage was small; from 1894 to 1923 it was high; and from 1923 to 1938, low. The growth in real wage again was high during the period from 1938 to 1973; but since 1979, there has been almost no growth.

SPECULATION IN PHYSICAL ASSET CYCLES

The economic long wave primarily results from major shifts both in physical capital construction and in prices of physical assets. Speculation in physical assets increases during peaks in the economic long wave. Figure 4 shows the price of agricultural land from 1916 to 1934, with an index value of 100 at the peak in 1920, a rise to a peak, a fall-off in the 1920s, and then a fairly substantial drop in the 1930s. Figure 5 is the corresponding chart for agricultural land from 1977 to the present; land values peaked in 1980 and began a downturn in a pattern similar to the 1920s chart. I anticipate that the low point in farm land values will occur around 1995. The value of agricultural land is now approximately half of what it was at the peak. The official statistics underestimate the actual decline.

Agricultural land typically has been the earliest of the speculative frenzies during a long-wave peak. Speculation then moves from one physical asset market to another. The last speculative burst appears to be in the equity market. This speculative increase in prices arises from changes in real interest rates. Near the peak, land values rise only because the value is rising, not because there is any increase in economic merit. At the 1980 peak in land prices, the interest paid on an investment in agricultural

FIGURE 4. Agricultural land values, 1916-1934

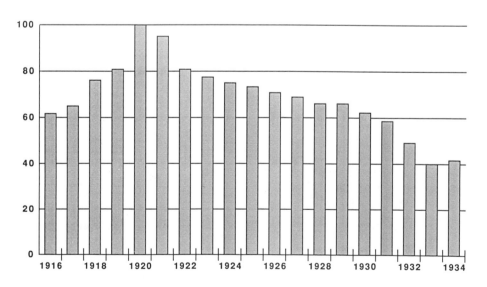

Agricultural Land Price Index
1920 = 100

Source: MIT System Dynamics Group

FIGURE 5. Agricultural land values after 1977

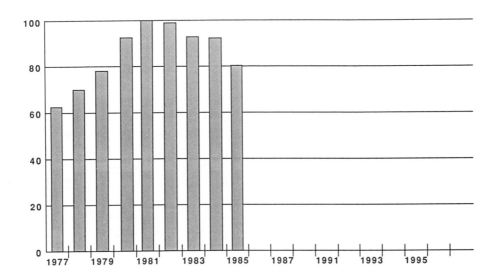

Agricultural Land Price Index
1981 = 100

FIGURE 6. Real interest rate on farm land

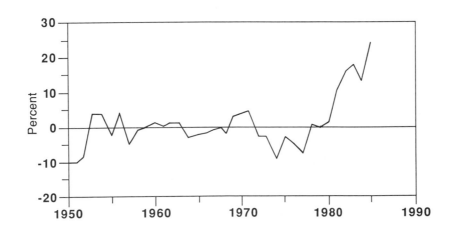

Source: MIT System Dynamics Group

land was as much as five times the earning capacity of the land, even for land with no development potential. The price was going up because the price was going up. Land was seen as a wonderful inflation hedge. Everyone was encouraged to buy land, because it was a way to protect against inflation and, for a certain amount of time, it was. As shown in Figure 6, real interest on farm land was negative in the 1970s. One could buy land with borrowed money, and, at the end of a year, sell the land, pay off the loan and the interest, and be 10 percent ahead. Speculative price rises continue until the price becomes absurd in terms of the underlying earning capacity of the asset. When some people cease buying and the price stabilizes, there is no reason for price to be so high. As soon as price starts to fall, the real interest rate (the bank interest minus inflation or the interest rate plus deflation) moves up into the range of 25 to 30 percent. Under such circumstances, few want to buy. Then, the foreclosures and forced sales push prices further down, so that deflation becomes higher until land values become absurdly low. At that point, buyers will intervene and stop the decline.

BUSINESS CYCLES: CAPACITY AND LABOR

Industrial capacity and labor also exhibit cycles. Figure 7 shows industrial capacity and usage of capital plant from 1960 to the present. The figure illustrates a growing amplitude of business cycles and a growing wedge of unused capacity between the two curves. The increase in unused capacity is a great deal larger than this figure shows, however, because the definition of capacity has been changing. If one had inquired in 1950 what percentage of plant capacity was utilized, the answer would often have been a percentage of a three-shift operation. Today, the answer would be a percentage of a one-shift operation. In other words, there may have been as much as a three-to-one change in the concept of capacity over several decades. We have been moving toward a concept of capacity that enables us to work conveniently in the daytime, whereas previously we worked around the clock.

Figure 8 illustrates the historical unemployment rate. Each business cycle recession since 1965 has shown a higher unemployment rate than its predecessor. We are moving into a

---

FIGURE 7. **Capacity, output, unused capacity, and increasing amplitude of business cycles**

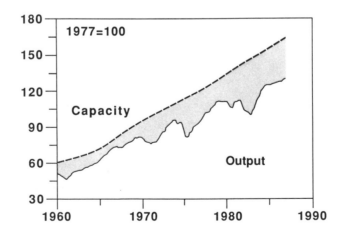

7/1

Source: MIT System Dynamics Group

FIGURE 8. Rising trend in unemployment

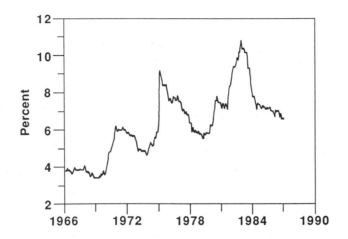

FIGURE 9. Computer simulation: business cycles superimposed on one economic long wave

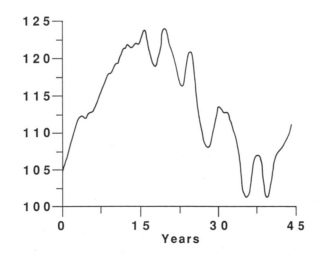

Source: MIT System Dynamics Group

period of more excess manufacturing capacity and more excess labor. This permits business cycles to manifest their full amplitude, because it is possible to overproduce in the recoveries— one could not have done that in the 1960s—after which a sharper cutback to rebalance inventories accentuates the downturn.

EVIDENCE OF THE LONG WAVE

There was a belief in the 1960s that business cycles had disappeared. Conferences were held on such subjects as "Where has the business cycle gone?" and "The death of the business cycle," up until business cycles began to come back with considerable vigor. The mild business cycles in the 1960s were a consequence of expansion of the long wave. When there is limited capacity in both labor and capital, business-cycle expansions are restrained. In a downturn, excess demand prevents serious recessions. During the long-wave expansion, it is not possible to overproduce on upturns of the business cycle, and there is an excess underlying demand to absorb the downturns, so business cycles are squeezed out on both the top and the bottom.

Figure 9 portrays a computer simulation from the National Model. There are no policy changes here, only an interplay between one economic long-wave and superimposed business cycles. Business cycles are suppressed during the long-wave expansion and become substantially more pronounced during the long-wave downturn.

Most people believe that the 1930s were a unique time of bank failures but that is hardly the complete picture. Table 3, shows that between 1910 and 1919, there were about 850 bank failures; from 1920 to 1929, there were 5882. In other words, the bank failure rate increased nearly sevenfold between those two decades. From 1930 to 1939, there were 9500 bank failures—an increase of only 60 percent over the previous decade. Most of these failures occurred in 1933 and 1934, but the rise of bank failures began long before general awareness that a major economic dislocation was on the way.

TABLE 3. Bank Failure Rates:

1910–1919:	849 banks
1920–1929:	5882 banks
1930–1939:	9506 banks

Source: MIT System Dynamics Group

Figure 10 illustrates the recent history of bank failures. From 1950 to 1980, failures were usually less than 10 per year, increasing slightly during recessions, and always decreasing again in recoveries. But in the 1982 recession, bank failures increased substantially, and did not decrease in the ensuing recovery; instead they continued to climb. This raises the question of what will occur in the next substantial recession.

There are other interesting patterns of behavior that go with the economic long wave. Figure 11 illustrates the history of corporate mergers, which peak at the end of long-wave expansions. The figure shows peaks in the early 1890s and the 1920s; mergers are peaking again now. I believe there is an underlying reason for merger patterns. In the build-up period, as in the 1950s and 1960s, money was being used to build physical capital plant. Then, we were short of physical capital plant. As one approaches excess capital plant levels—which now is evident in nearly all industries—there is no desire to build more capital plant. The depreciation cash flows that would have been reinvested in physical plant are no longer wanted for that purpose. Money from depreciation cash flows is available for other uses. Also, government, seeing a decline in physical investment, tends to make credit readily available in an effort to encourage more physical investment even when almost every investor is overinvested.

These two sources of money—the depreciation cash flow and the added borrowing—tend to be directed toward financial assets and mergers and acquisitions. Corporations should be using the depreciation cash flows to pay back the earnings that were withheld during the capital buildup to their stockholders. But few corporate managements want to do that directly, so they do it indirectly, by buying the stock of other companies, and paying their depreciation cash flows to the stockholders of other companies rather than their own.

There is a common belief that the service sector is immune to economic adversities. Indeed, services are little affected by short-term business cycles. The service sector is highly vulnerable to a downturn in the economic long wave, however. This may be seen in the layoffs of municipal employees in 1982, and also in the unemployment that quickly develops on Wall Street during such a downturn period. America, much to its detriment, has allowed manufactur-

FIGURE 10.   Recent bank failures

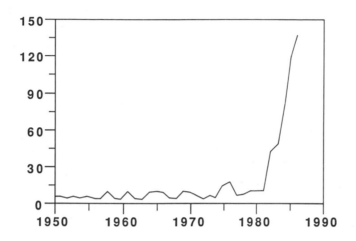

FIGURE 11.   Corporate mergers since 1895

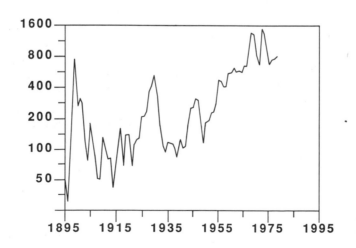

Source: MIT System Dynamics Group

ing to move to other countries. This country will return to manufacturing when unemployment reaches high levels. It is likely that high unemployment will come primarily from the service sector.

OUR CURRENT POSITION IN THE LONG WAVE

I believe that the peak of the long wave was in the late 1970s, and that the low point will be in the mid-1990s. The pattern of an increasing amplitude of short-term business cycles with each recession bringing higher unemployment peaks will probably continue for two more business cycle downturns. The second business cycle downturn, in the mid-1990s, will be the one that shakes out the imbalances in our economic system. Those imbalances are substantial. There are obvious debt imbalances. For example, the Latin American debt must be defaulted—there is nothing else to do with it. I understand that the Latin American debt is greater than the net worth of the entire American banking system. The agricultural land debt in this country is greater than the Latin American debt, and is just as vulnerable. The junk bond debt is about equal to the debt of Brazil, and a great deal of it cannot survive a severe recession.

There are other kinds of imbalances as well. There is excess physical capital plant, which is overpriced. It must be discarded before rebuilding can take place. There are imbalances of the labor force in capital-producing sectors. Many capital-producing jobs are finished for the time being. When those jobs come back, they will not be for the same people in the same locations. Instead, new companies in new geographical locations will be making new kinds of equipment. In the last downturn, firms and people making steam locomotives gave way to different firms and people making aircraft. We can anticipate a transition in technology of nearly that same magnitude between now and the year 2010.

Another way to look at the economic long wave is to superimpose several short-term business cycles on top of each other, as shown in Figure 12. In this figure, business cycles all have been started at their low points and recalibrated to 100 percent, so that they can be placed on top of one another and each pattern observed rela-tive to the others. The very long-term growth trend of 3.4 percent—the average growth trend for the past 185 years—has been taken out. With the very long trend removed, two modes of change are left: the short-term business cycle, and the economic long wave. The first major business cycle, from 1961 to 1970, rose and declined to a value that was above the beginning; I would interpret the higher end point as representing the still expanding economic long wave. The second cycle rises, but falls lower than its beginning point—lower relative to that 3.4 percent growth trend. The third cycle rises, lasts longer than its predecessor, and falls still lower. The current cycle is represented by the heavy line.

Most people believe that the present business cycle has shown an unusually strong recovery; that is not supported by this figure. The current cycle rises to a peak slightly higher than the others, but this is hardly more than random variation; and, according to this figure from which the long-term growth trend has been removed, the peak of this business cycle occurred earlier than peaks of previous cycles. This is a different presentation than used by the National Bureau of Economic Research (NBER). The NBER leaves in the 3.4 percent very long growth trend, and so they have not seen the peak yet. Viewed without the long-term growth trend, however, the peak of this particular business cycle has passed.

Figure 13 illustrates the relationship of innovation to the economic long wave, beginning in the 1700s. The shaded strips are the great depressions, and the solid black line shows technological innovations. The solid line does not indicate inventions, but rather the time at which new technologies became an important part of commerce. These are major innovations, such as the change from railroads to aircraft, or from radio to television—the big shifts from old technologies to new. The upsurges in innovation occur during major depressions.

In successive long-wave downturns there have been changes in energy sources: the shift from wood to coal and from coal to oil. The end of the oil supply is fairly close. It is unclear whether the present downturn will be the time for change from oil to another energy source, or whether oil can last one more cycle before being replaced.

In the long-wave decline that is now under-

FIGURE 12.   Superimposed business cycles with real GNP trend of 3.4 percent removed

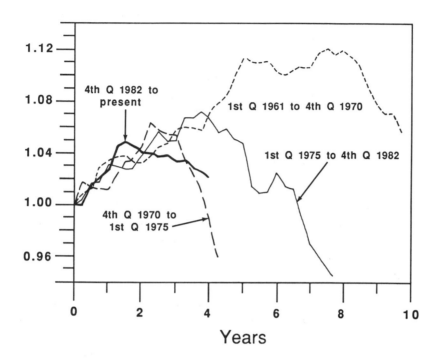

FIGURE 13.   Major innovations during and after great depressions

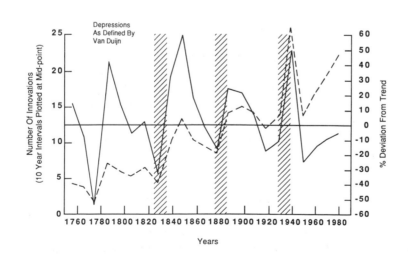

Source: MIT System Dynamics Group

way, there is potential for another change in energy source as well as other major technological changes. This window of opportunity for technological change will create new industries during the next two decades. These new innovations will be built around inventions that have existed for as many as 100 years. Many new ideas will not succeed because their time has not come. For example, the logic for the modern digital computer was written up in the mid 1800s; but its time did not come until the technology to build such a computer and the economic need coincided. At this stage, however, the challenge is not to invent them, but to pick and choose among them.

I feel that the present economic cross-currents are largely a consequence of our having entered another major downturn in the economic long wave. Traditionally, these downturns have been periods of major deflation. A great deal of economic stress has resulted from the debt-deflation spirals. As debt was repaid to banks, repayment collapsed the money supply, reduced prices, and made the remaining debt progressively harder to pay. Even as debt was reduced, it became more and more burdensome. That may or may not happen during this downturn. For the first time, there is a possibility of major money infusion into the system, so the debt deflation spiral may not be as severe. But that is unclear. There is very little the Federal Reserve can do by making credit available if people do not want to borrow. Those who are borrowing to buy either physical or financial assets will stop doing so when prices begin to fall. The collapse of the money supply may be fairly rapid in spite of the Federal

Reserve. There is the possibility of feeding money into the system through fiscal policies, with the threat of igniting an inflation further down the road. I feel that it is possible to have a physical depression accompanied by inflation— in other words, unemployment along with inflation. There also is the possibility of a deflation followed by a runaway inflation, which would give us the worst of both worlds.

If one must choose between inflation or deflation, the latter probably is the better choice, because it will be over sooner, the excess debt will be defaulted faster, and the deck will be cleared for a recovery more quickly than if we put off the day of reckoning. At present, we temporize on the Latin American debts, we loan money for them to pay interest, and say the assets are still good. We do the same thing in the banking system with respect to the value of both agricultural and urban land. In the physical economy, there is a high probability that excess manufacturing capacity will not be fully utilized. There will be rising unemployment.

The financial markets will also be affected. If I picked articles from the financial press of the late 1920s and presented them here with the implication that they were taken from yesterday's paper, no one would know the difference. The attitudes of the financial community of that time were the same as at present—the get-rich-quick syndrome, the insistence that there cannot be problems because the securities are safe, the expectation that sovereign nations do not default on their debts, and that Latin America has many assets and resources that can be used to pay off debts. This was all said before in the 1920s.

Question and Answer Session

QUESTION: How should one hedge against a long-wave downturn?

FORRESTER: My choice is short-term Treasuries. Long-term Treasuries are affected by the growing national debt, which is doubling almost every administration. The U.S. debt is beginning to be similar to the Latin American debt, but we will not face up to that immediately. We must default it, or inflate out of it. The recent behavior of the equity market is similar to the process that drove agricultural land prices up, devastating American farmers. Those who borrowed at the peak are in great trouble. Those who did not are in relatively good shape. The equity market will be the same. It can run up as long as people believe it will run up, even though it is entirely out of touch with the underlying fundamentals. And when that confidence breaks, the market can come down very fast.

QUESTION: How do you respond to critics who say that your model is an attempt to fit theory to past data rather than a predictive instrument?

FORRESTER: It is not an attempt to fit theory to past data. I had never heard of the economic long wave when we started developing the national model. We discovered, however, that as we linked the ordinary short-run policies that are practiced in industry and banking together, the model produced this long-wave activity. Then we discovered the vast literature on the economic long wave. There are hundreds of papers on the economic long wave that essentially are out of sight as far as America is concerned; they are mostly in Europe, and have been forgotten. There is considerable literature on the behavior of the long wave, but nowhere is there a really plausible theory. You cannot put this complicated situation together without a computer simulation model. It is not possible to put all the pieces together in your head and understand the implications and interactions. There are a number of policies—for example, investment and pricing—which are quite mundane when they are observed individually. The surprising thing is what happens when they begin to interact with one another.

QUESTION: Would you bet on inflation or deflation?

FORRESTER: I said four years ago that I thought there was a 60 percent chance of runaway inflation, a 30 percent chance of deflation and not more than a 10 percent chance of steering a way between the two. I would say now that the deflationary forces have become ascendant, and that probably we have a 70 percent chance of deflation, with severe deflation in certain places. The agricultural land situation is strongly deflationary, as is the urban land in some places—I believe rents on office buildings in many cities are down 20 percent or so, while the corresponding value of building has not been adjusted on the books. The disinflation that Washington is so proud of is really a deflation. In the past few years we have seen things that would have been absolutely impossible in the 1970s—for example, to give back the reduced wage payments in a lot of industries. There were a lot of people at that time who said it could not happen. It is also happening in government with municipal employees. So I am more inclined to believe in deflation in the short run. Beyond that, the probability of extreme inflation remains, because of the government deficit and the government debt situation.

QUESTION: Did Keynesianism, as new economic theory, play a role in defining the problems of the 1930s, and therefore solving them, or is the long wave so certain that no new thinking is required to exit from the trough?

FORRESTER: I do not think that the Keynesian movement had much to do with the situation in the 1930s; we would have come out of it anyway. Keynesian economics is given credit for the very mild business cycles in the 1950s and 1960s, but its effects did not persist afterwards. When people do not understand the economic long wave, they often take actions based on short-term pressures that in fact make the process worse.

I think we are headed for some sort of restructuring. We must do something about the debt, the excess manufacturing capacity, and the shift of employment to new industries. A public understanding of what is happening is very important, because otherwise there is a great risk of recrimination—Group A blaming Group B. This phenomenon is not the fault of the Democrats, the Republicans, the bankers, the farmers, or any one group; it is a consequence of what everyone wanted to do at the time that the foundation was being laid. Suppose, for example, we could have greatly reduced the overshoot that we are in now, and thereby reduced the decline that would be forthcoming, or that we could have prevented the severity of the overshoot and decline if we had engaged in extremely tight monetary policy beginning in 1960 or 1965, and sustained it for 20 years. Where was the constituency for doing that at that time? I do not think you can name a single one. It would take a political understanding great enough to support something of that nature to overcome the dynamic that we are talking about, however. This dynamic is built into the psychology of people; it is built into the fact that we have a society that produces through the use of capital plant; it is built into the financial markets and what they can do to shift the financial capital from one place to another; it is built into the length of time it takes to build up expectations and shatter those expectations. There are a number of components of the dynamic that in fact do not change over time. The generating mechanism of this long wave does not really depend very much on any of the changes that have occurred within our economy over the past 100 years. Therefore, we must have a change in understanding, in attitudes, in policies, and be willing to sustain them if we want to have any effect on the future. For example, coming out of the 1930s, banks inaugurated policies such as no short-term construction loans on office buildings unless the building was 80 percent rented before construction began. That kind of regulation was kept in place for 20 or 30 years when it was not needed, and then abandoned in the decade when it was needed. It requires two or three generations of bankers and managers before the cycle is repeated: they think they have discovered growth forever, so they give up the lessons learned previously and fall into the same attitudes that eventually lead to the same problems.

Indexing Fixed-Income Investments

Frederic A. Nelson III

In discussing the indexation of fixed-income investments, one must consider the evolution of bond indexing, the current size of the market, the choice of an index, and trading techniques. It is also instructive to contrast bond indexation with its counterpart on the equity side.

Although the popularity of passive equity investing has fostered the growth of bond index funds, the origins of the two are dissimilar in many respects. Equity indexing gained momentum due to the large body of academic research on the efficient market hypothesis. The Capital Asset Pricing Model (CAPM) framework is used to test the existence of an efficient market basket of securities, typically proxied by the S&P 500. The academic interest and the choice of the S&P 500 naturally suggested S&P 500 index funds. On the fixed-income side, there has been less academic interest. The CAPM framework was not applied to bonds, and there was no suggestion that an index of all publicly-traded bonds, weighted by amount outstanding, was an efficient portfolio to hold. This lack of theoretical support was augmented by a general lack of interest in bonds by plan sponsors. Equities— and selecting managers to manage them—were the exciting area. The only thing duller than choosing fixed-income managers was choosing a bond index fund.

That is not to say that people were not interested in bond indexing prior to the first funds in 1981. Before that time, it was known as customized bond indexing, or immunization and dedication. The greater precision of these passive strategies absorbed the existing demand for indexing.

These impediments have largely been overcome. The current popularity of indexation is evidenced by the magnitude of assets under management. At the end of 1986, the size of indexation activity was approximately $30 billion in straight indexation, with another $20 billion in customized (or enhanced return) index funds. The bulk of passively-managed assets, over $100 billion, still remain in dedicated and immunized portfolios.

THE CASE FOR BOND INDEXATION

The case for indexation is very straightforward. First, it provides a structured approach to investment in the fixed-income market. Bond indexes allow plan sponsors to target their allocation to the market more efficiently than they could by hiring an array of managers, each with specific guidelines. Second, index investment management fees are 80 percent lower than active fixed-income fee schedules. The reduced fee argument is very much in line with the rationale for equity indexing. The third and most dominating argument also parallels the rationale for equity indexing: indexes historically have had good performance relative to active management.

Figure 1, an SEI chart, outlines bond industry performance. The figure plots the Salomon Brothers Broad Investment Grade (BIG) Index and the Shearson Lehman Corporate/Government Index on the ranking of active managers' returns.

The indexes have been in the first or second quartile in the one, three, and five-year periods. The index returns would be difficult to match with a real portfolio; transaction costs exist, and the maturing aspect of bonds would create turnover. Yet one must remember that the active manager returns are misleading due to survivorship bias. Good managers remain in the SEI survey; poor managers drop out as they are fired or stop reporting returns. In effect, the bonds' indexes have performed well compared to the best of active managers.

The case against indexation has been suggested already. The CAPM framework is not effective in assessing bonds, because in this context it is not clear that the bond market is an efficient portfolio. Even if one believes that the market is efficient, it is doubtful whether the Shearson or Salomon indexes represent the proper holdings for the average investor. For example, double counting occurs in bond indexes as illustrated by the case when both a Treasury bond and a corporate bond are in-

FIGURE 1.   Managed bond portfolios: Total fund rates of return

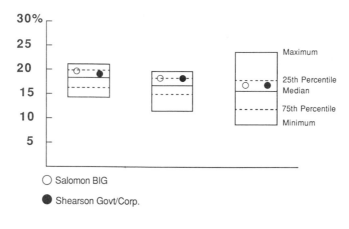

	Five Years*	Three Years*	One Year
25th Percentile	18.4	17.4	16.7
Median	17.5	16.0	14.7
75th Percentile	15.8	14.2	12.0
Salomon BIG	18.2	17.5	15.4
Shearson Govt/Corp	17.9	17.2	15.5

*Annualized returns SEI Data

Sources: Salomon Brothers Inc., Shearson Lehman Brothers, Inc., and SEI Data.

cluded in an index, even though the Treasury bond is set aside in a trust to defease a corporate bond (in reality the defeased portion of each issue should be weighted zero). Thus a legitimate bond index is more elusive than the efficient portfolio on the equity side.

A more subjective argument, somewhat in line with the efficiency aspect of a particular index, is that none of the published bond indexes reflect a return pattern that the investor really desires. A bond index is said to react like a portfolio insurance strategy, because of the inverse relationship between yield and duration. For example, if interest rates rise and bond prices fall, investors might want to maintain or even increase their exposure to interest-rate changes, implying a constant portfolio duration or increase in portfolio duration. The increase in yields actually would be associated with a decrease in the duration of an indexed portfolio, however, because of the mechanical inverse relationship between yield levels and duration. Although such a move—to reduce the risk exposure of the portfolio after it declines in value—is consistent with portfolio insurance

strategies, it is not consistent with the usual notion of an indexed portfolio as one that maintains constant risk exposure over time.

The objection to indexed portfolios centers on whether an investor wants to reduce duration when rates are high, and increase duration when rates are low. This is akin to the argument against equity portfolio insurance: that one sells low and buys high. The response is the same for equities and bonds.

The high stock price is relative to the past; it is not high relative to the future, which cannot be predicted. The high interest rate also is high only on a historical—not a prospective—basis.

The portfolio insurance objection may be taken to a deeper level. The bond index replicates a call pattern. There is a cost to owning this call (insurance) and the long-run-minded plan sponsor should not forego these returns. Instead, the sponsor should follow a strategy which maintains a constant duration of the bond portfolio, lengthening duration as interest rates rise. This is similar to selling portfolio insurance.

This approach, however, does not dominate

a bond indexing strategy. Although the term "convexity" has gained popularity recently, people have long been aware of the implicit call characteristics of bonds, and have chosen to buy them despite (or because of) this. To the extent that the duration of the bond index drops as interest rates rise, it may only offset the falling duration of the pension plan's liabilities. Actually, yield and duration in the index historically have not had a strong inverse relation. Figure 2 demonstrates that the Shearson Lehman index duration remained fairly stable from 1975 through 1984, despite large changes in yield. The implicit call aspect in the index may be modified by increasing the weight of bond sectors in which yield and duration are positively related—such as mortgage-backed and corporate issues.

Finally, it should be noted that a constant duration strategy is not the neutral position. In effect, one follows the actions of a seller of a call option. In a market where interest rates rise in a straight line, a constant duration strategy would lead to continued losses as duration is extended. One might need a strong stomach to follow such a strategy.

All of this gets away from the fundamental reason why people are adopting bond index funds—performance. A customized passive approach (dedication) might make more sense for a plan sponsor; but today, index funds are chosen as an alternative to active managers, not to dedication. On this level the bond indexes have proven to be well structured and good portfolio managers on a return basis.

CONSIDERATIONS IN THE CHOICE OF AN INDEX

The choice of the index must be considered. The selection has two aspects: the components of the index, and the vendor or the benchmark actually supplied by a broker/dealer. One might look at any number of published broad market indexes—the Salomon Brothers BIG Index, the Shearson Lehman Corporate/Government Index, or one of the Merrill Lynch indexes—all of which measure exposure to the total debt market. It might be more important to focus on the subindexes, however, and to choose an index that is more appropriate for an individual plan. Also, it is important to consider the different maturity ranges—short, intermediate, or long. The sector chosen could be quite important as well, as some segments may not be appropriate for all portfolios.

It is difficult to determine the most appropriate index for a client. The decision on whether one should have government, corporate, or mortgage-backed securities in the index is influenced by the fact that all bond indexes are imperfect representations of the fixed-income market. If one wishes to do market timing, then a bond index that focuses on the government market might be quite effective, because it is possible to move in and out of that market

FIGURE 2. Shearson Lehman Government/Corporate Index yield and duration, 1975–1986

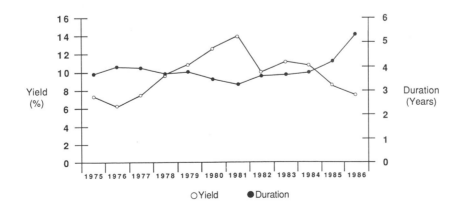

Source: Shearson Lehman Brothers, Inc.

inexpensively. Alternatively, if active managers have been hired to make quality or sector bets, a government bond index fund is attractive to provide liquidity for the portfolio and save on investment management fees, giving the more specialized pieces to the active managers. Similarly, a corporation may decide that it does not want to buy bonds in its own industry.

A great deal of furor has arisen in the past several years over the matter of vendors. Salomon Brothers challenged the industry when they introduced the BIG Index, because they identified 22 percent of the market that was important—such as mortgage-backed securities—but had not been included in other indexes. Figure 3 illustrates the total rate of return for the BIG Index and the Corporate/Government. There is not a great deal of difference in historical performance between these two indexes, despite sector differences.

In the same context, one must determine whether a particular dealer is better at calculating an index. Figure 4 depicts the BIG Index versus the Shearson Lehman Aggregate. Once again, they mirror each other almost perfectly, except in some of the early years. This suggests that it is not essential to base one's choice of an index on the way the numbers are calculated; however, there are other considerations. For example, there are some nuances in how coupon reinvestment occurs in the respective indexes.

PERFORMANCE MEASUREMENT

Performance measurement may be a very difficult issue. Pricing and measurement error present problems. Differences in prices may make a portfolio look very good or very bad relative to a benchmark. In addition, large cash flows in a portfolio might create problems for the performance measurement system, which is geared to dollar-weighting intramonth rates of return. Accurate measurement is extremely important as the industry moves to incentive-based fees. It is ironic that we cannot measure accurately within plus or minus 20 basis points, yet millions can be gained or lost on our precision.

After the appropriate index is chosen, the portfolio itself must be constructed using various indexing techniques. A number of models are available that take into account the duration of a portfolio, the cash flow patterns of the portfolio, quality, sector, coupon, and particularly sinking fund and call provisions within the index. Two models are prevalent: stratified sampling, and risk optimization.

The key feature of the stratified sampling technique is that it is independent of historical returns. The technique involves identifying those characteristics that are important to bond return and risk—such as maturity, sector, and quality—and creating various cells from the intersections of these states. Bonds are then selected in such a way that the portfolio weighting in each cell is equal to the index weight in the cell. Table 1 shows the results of breaking the various stratifications into subdivisions. This breakdown example involves four maturity ranges, five types of sectors, quality AAA through BBB, call or no-call, and sinking fund or no sinking fund categories. There are 416 intersections, or cells, in this case. Presumably, one would want to select bonds to represent each of those cells.

The use of a risk model is very different. It is dependent on historical return relationships. The approach involves identifying those factors that are important to bond risk and return, measuring the volatility of each factor, assessing the co-variability among the factors, and then applying an optimization model. Issues are chosen that will minimize the tracking deviation versus the index, while maximizing yield.

Either of these two models can produce good results, but they have different strengths and weaknesses. First, there is the question of whether historical estimates introduce a bias. The sampling model would not have that problem, whereas the risk optimization model would. For some bonds, even if the model is correct on average, bad data or the fact that history may not repeat itself makes some bond risk estimates too high and others too low. The problem is that the model focuses on minimizing risk versus the index. It will tend to select those bonds for which the risk is most underestimated; however, this approach might introduce other problems into the portfolio.

The ability to make trade-offs is important in the choice of a model. Trade-offs may be made and quantified more easily with a risk-model approach than with the sampling approach. The cells are very rigid in the sampling technique; there is no sense of overweighting and under-

FIGURE 3. Salomon BIG Index and Shearson Lehman Government/Corporate
Index returns

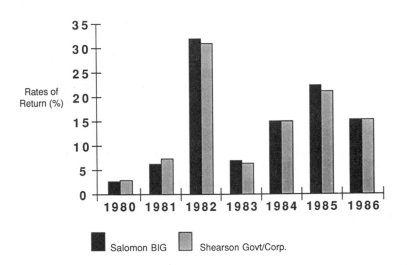

FIGURE 4. Salomon BIG Index and Shearson Lehman Aggregate Index returns

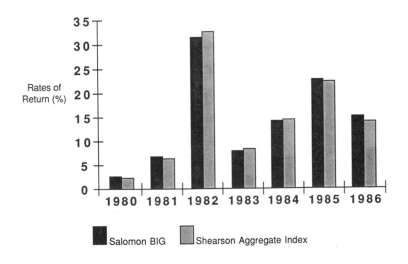

Sources: Salomon Brothers, Inc., Shearson Lehman Brothers, Inc.

TABLE 1. Potential Subdivisions of a Government/Corporate Index

Stratifications	Sub-Divisions
Maturity	4
Sector	5
Quality	4
Call/No Call	2
Sinking Fund/No SF	2
Coupon Level	2
Cells	416

Source: Bankers Trust Company

weighting, because there is no frame of reference, no risk model. Furthermore, tracking error predictions is not possible for the sampling technique, whereas it is possible for the risk model. It is important to point out that the sampling technique will have more bonds if the goal is to track well.

Pricing is another important aspect of indexing. Treasury bond prices are generally very good, but with corporate bonds it is difficult to tell which prices are accurate. Therefore, when these prices are entered into a yield-maximization model, there may be problems. In addition, there may be a lack of liquidity even if the prices are good. Therefore, to unite the model with reality, one must create a subset of bond prices that are trader priced. This is accomplished by working with traders and dealers, identifying those bonds that are available and appear to be legitimately priced, and putting them into the model. Once a solution is created, traders must review it for reasonableness; then trading may take place.

Trading style must be established. The typical alternatives are program trading and the more traditional trading involving competitive versus selective bids and offers. Program trading—trading a large dollar amount of securities

in a short period of time—has been popular on the equity side, but it does not work as well on the bond side. Securities firms are reluctant to submit bids on a specific package of securities, because it is difficult for them to judge the prices they will have to pay for the individual issues.

In some cases, the more traditional types of trading—seeking selective bids—may be more appropriate. If there is an issue in one's portfolio which a broker has in inventory, then one can go directly to that broker. Competitive bids may be very effective on the other issues in a portfolio, however. Bond futures also may be used to get exposure to the market, at least with respect to interest-rate risk.

The Treasury market provides an example of the value of compeititive bids. One might think that Treasury issues trade in a narrow range. Table 2 presents actual competitive offers on Treasuries. The difference in basis points between the aggregate for each broker and the lowest price ranges between 26 basis points and 9 basis points. This shows that there was a potential gain from doing competitive offerings on these issues, even though they were fairly liquid and should trade in a tight band.

Analysts' ability to forecast interest rates of sector/quality spreads should make the bond market efficient, but things may still be done to enhance returns. There is far more turnover in a bond index fund than in an equity index fund, because in the bond fund, issues that go below a one-year maturity are taken out of the portfolio and replaced with new issues. Assuming that a manager does not have confidence in an ability to forecast interest rates or changes in sector spreads, one strategy is to supply liquidity to the market. By playing on clientele effect—perhaps supplying bonds to Japanese investors who are seeking particular issues—and recreat

TABLE 2. Competitive Offers on U.S. Treasury Issues

Quantity	Bond	Shearson	Salomon	Drexel	Refco	Merrill	Best
($000)							
9,000	10 ½ of '95	118.50	117.84	118.06	118.34	118.11	117.84
2,670	11 ¼ of '15	138.50	138.50	138.38	138.03	138.50	138.03
1,335	10 ¾ of '05	127.56	127.56	127.56	127.53	127.59	127.53
9,900	10 ⅝ of '15	131.81	131.66	131.62	131.52	131.63	131.52
13,650	10 ⅛ of '93	113.38	113.41	113.28	113.33	113.47	113.28
Total Cost ($000)		44,591	44,520	44,515	44,528	44,550	44,475
% Difference from Best		+.26	+.12	+.09	+.17	+.10	—

Source: Bankers Trust Company

ing a similar position with the other bonds, one can trade on the margin and reduce the dead-weight loss of the portfolio due to turnover.

One thing that bond fund managers like about active bond portfolios is the fees. Thus, the number of enhanced index funds will increase. With an active bond management process in place, one can use the bond indexing technology, particularly if a risk model is used to measure risk, and stay within the client-defined constraints. Performance-based fees capitalize on this possibility. Bond index fund managers, believing they can add value, per-haps should be willing to make the move to enhanced index funds.

CONCLUSION

Bond indexing differs significantly from equity indexing. It lacks a good deal of the theoretical support. The lack of a bond pricing tape and the nuances of trading make bond indexing techni-cally more difficult. Yet, like equity indexing, it offers a structured approach with good relative performance and low fees. Look for bond index-ing and the related return enhancements—the bells and whistles—to grow in the future.

Securitization Strategies

Anthony V. Dub

The market for asset-backed securities is relatively new. Companies have sold receivables on a private basis in the past, but until two years ago no one had attempted to offer publicly securities backed by assets.

The first such transaction, in March 1985, was a Sperry Lease Finance Corporation offering that was backed by computer leases. In early 1985, several other issues appeared, primarily backed by auto loans. By the end of 1985, the market value of such offerings was $1.2 billion. In 1986, volume soared to about $10 billion. This level of activity has attracted a great deal of attention. The market is continuing to grow and to provide interesting investment alternatives.

WHY SECURITIZE ASSETS?

Companies may want to securitize assets for several reasons. First, asset securitization is an alternative to direct issuance of debt securities. Second, asset securitization improves asset/liability matching, particularly for finance companies. Treasurers spend a great deal of time trying to match assets and liabilities; it is virtually impossible, however, to get a perfect matching of assets and liabilities because the prepayment characteristics of the assets are often unknown. A good way to deal with the problem is to avoid it by passing the risk on to someone else.

The third reason is lower costs. The issuance of asset-backed securities often appears to cost more than direct issuance of conventional debt. For example, when General Motors Acceptance Corporation (GMAC) first started issuing these securities, they might have been priced at 75 basis points over the Treasury rate, whereas a corporate debt issue by GMAC might have been 60 or 65 basis points over the Treasury rate. But when the cost of equity needed to underlay the conventional debt issue is added, a significantly lower cost of funding is achieved by the asset-backed securities sale than with most alternatives. This is because asset-backed securities result in a sale of assets and, unlike traditional debt securities, require little or no equity to support them.

THE MARKET FOR ASSET-BACKED SECURITIES

The following statistics will provide some idea of the potential market for asset-backed securities. Total consumer installment credit outstanding is currently $595 billion—approximately one-fourth the size of the mortgage market. The automobile market accounts for the largest portion, at $242 billion, credit card paper represents $128 billion, and mobile homes $25 billion; the remaining $200 billion is composed of miscellaneous types of consumer loans. One might think that the potential market for asset-backed securities is small because the market itself is so much smaller than the mortgage market. Two things must be considered. First, this $595 billion is only consumer installment debt; statistics on nonconsumer or corporate installment securities are unavailable. Second, most of this debt is relatively short term. A typical auto loan matures in three to four years; a typical mortgage has a maturity of 20 to 30 years. So the potential market for asset-backed securities could evolve quite rapidly because of the two- or three-year turnover.

ASSET CHARACTERISTICS

The ideal asset for securitization would have several characteristics. First, it would have predictable cash flows. In trying to create a fixed-income instrument, predictable cash flows are easier to securitize than unpredictable cash flows. Low late payment levels, low net credit losses, and high-quality assets are necessary. The asset should have total principal amortization over its life. If it has a balloon at the end, it becomes more difficult to securitize. The average life should be greater than one year, because these transactions take three to six months to structure. It is senseless to spend three months structuring something that will mature in four months. Diverse obligors offer the advantages of creating a pool with some credit diversification. High liquidation value is an important characteristic—as typified by the automobile paper market, where the automobile may be liquidated if necessary. Of course, high utility of the underlying asset is also important, because it does not make sense to securitize something that cannot be used by someone else.

Asset-related securities usually are structured in one of four ways. Asset-backed certificates, commonly referred to as *pass-throughs*, are the traditional form issued under a grantor trust, and are very common in the mortgage market. Asset-backed notes, commonly referred to as *pay-throughs*, are basically collateralized debt. There is some advantaqge to such notes from an investor's point of view, because the actual cash payments may be manipulated; for example, the security may have quarterly payments instead of monthly payments.

The remaining two forms are asset-backed obligations and credit card asset-backed securities. Last year a company called Asset Backed Securities Corporation (ABSC) had a $4 billion issue; this was the largest such issue ever in the United States. These were asset-backed obligations. They were multi-tranched—in this case, three tranches, paying quarterly. A unique feature of that issue was that there was absolutely no prepayment uncertainty. In the ABSC issue, the prepayment risk was handled in the structure, and the bonds sold to investors had no prepayment risk whatsoever. For the first time,

a structure was created that absorbed prepayment risk in itself.

The latest generation is credit card asset-backed securities. The first public sale of credit card receivables—a $400 million transaction—was done by Bank of America in the spring of 1987. These securities are interesting from an investment point of view, because for the first 18 months there is an interest-only period; no principal will be repaid. Principal will then be repaid over a period of about five months. So the duration is very consistent; at any time, one knows almost exactly what the average life will be.

INVESTMENT CONSIDERATIONS

With a market that is only 24 months old, it is important that, the securities be very high quality. In fact, all public asset-backed-security transactions to date have been rated AAA or AA. This is very similar to the precedent set in the early days of the mortgage market.

Asset-backed-security issues have two layers of credit. The first layer is the quality of the assets themselves. Normally, high-quality underlying assets are involved, and the credit of the obligors is examined, as in the case of automobile loans. Autos are readily marketable, and most Americans are reliable in paying their automobile loans on time. The second layer of credit arises from the credit enhancement. There are several ways to structure this, including recourse to the seller, overcollateralization, or a letter of credit or surety bond.

A second reason for the high credit quality is that asset-backed securities do not have event

TABLE 1. Prepayment Experience: Asset-Backed Securities vs. Collateralized Mortgage Obligations

GMAC 1985-A Grantor Trust, 48-Month Contracts

| | Interest Rate Environment | | |
Autombile Loan Coupon Rate	High 3/82 - 5/82	Low 3/83 - 5/83	Moderate 3/84 - 5/84
Less than 12%	1.50%	1.38%	1.20%
12% to 14%	1.37	1.35	1.34
Greater than 14%	1.37	1.50	1.55
Weighted Average	1.38	1.43	1.47

Note Assumes Absolute Prepayment Method
Source: First Boston Corporation

TABLE 2. Average Life and Duration: Asset-Backed Securities vs. Collaterized Mortgage Obligations

	Prepayment Rate (%)					
Absolute Model (%)	0.00	0.40	0.80	1.20	1.60	2.00
Average Life	2.26	2.11	1.97	1.82	1.68	1.53
Duration	2.00	1.88	1.76	1.64	1.52	1.40
Single Monthly Mortality Model (%)						
Average Life	5.90	2.33	1.40	0.99	0.77	0.63
Duration	4.25	2.00	1.27	0.93	0.73	0.60

Source: First Boston Corporation

risk. A number of companies that have issued A- or AA-rated securities have had problems and setbacks, and the securities have fallen to BBB or BB ratings. One of the nicer things about a grantor trust structure is that once everything is in place, there is not much that can happen to it. One cannot go out and do a leveraged buyout on it, or buy a company and ruin the ratings, and that has a significant amount of appeal to investors.

Asset-backed securities generally have more consistent prepayment experience than the typical mortgage-backed security. The data for asset-backed securities shown in Table 1 are drawn from a pool of General Motors Acceptance Corporation receivables. The table shows prepayment rates in three different interest-rate environments, using March through May in every period. Throughout the tables that appear in this presentation, the absolute prepayment model (Abs) is used for automobile receivables, and the Single Monthly Mortality model (SMM) is used for mortgage-backed securities. For example, 1.50 Abs means that in any month, it is

expected that 1.5 percent of the original number of automobile loans will prepay in that month. Table 1 shows that, generally speaking, the higher coupon auto receivables tend to prepay faster than those with a lower coupon.

Another interesting point is that prepayment experience is not consistently dependent on the interest-rate environment. For example, one would expect that, similar to the mortgage market, prepayments would be higher in a low interest-rate environment than in a high interest-rate environment. However, one finds this is not the case. People tend not to refinance automobile loans because of changes in interest rates, although they may prepay automobile loans to sell or because of an accident.

As a result, prepayment experience exhibits a level of consistency that is not found in the mortgage market. Table 2 shows what would happen to average life and duration with different prepayment assumptions. The first half of the table examines asset-backed securities. Using the absolute prepayment model, duration varies from 2 years to 1.4 years. Looking at the

TABLE 3. Positive Convexity: Asset-Backed Securities vs. Collateralized Mortgage Obligations

Interest-Rate Environment	Instantaneous Returns		
	CMO	Corporate Debenture	GMAC 1985-A
(basis points)			
+500	−14.81%	−7.55%	−8.09%
+300	−8.50	−4.64	−4.81
+100	−2.63	−1.60	−1.59
Unchanged	—	—	—
−100	+2.00	+1.58	+1.69
−300	+2.50	+4.88	+5.09
−500	+3.28	+8.34	+8.41

Source: First Boston Corporation

TABLE 4. Comparison of Yield Premia

| | Basis Points Over Treasury | | | | |
| | 1986 | | | | 1987 |
	1st Q	2nd Q	3rd Q	4th Q	1st Q*
2-Year GMAC	57	60	59	52	45
2-Year CMO	100	134	125	107	95
GMAC 1985-A	77	97	107	82	75
ABSC Class 1-B ABO	—	—	—	61	55
California Credit Card 1987-A	—	—	—	—	70

*Through March 9th
Source: First Boston Corporation

same statistics for the first tranche of a CMO, the duration ranges from 4.25 down to 0.60 years—a very significant change.

The differences in duration change imply substantial differences in convexity. Table 3 shows a comparison of mortgages, corporate debt, and typical asset-backed securities in scenarios where shortly after investment, there is

TABLE 5. The U.S. Public Asset-Backed Security Market

Date	Issuer	Amount	Lead Manager
1985		(millions)	
03/07	Sperry	$ 192	First Boston
05/15	Valley National	101	First Boston
05/15	Marine	60	Salomon
08/01	Home Federal	103	Salomon
09/12	Sperry	146	First Boston
12/12	GMAC	525	First Boston
12/13	Western Financial	110	Drexel
	Total	$ 1,237	
1986			
01/23	GMAC	$ 424	First Boston
04/16	GMAC	1,049	First Boston
06/18	Empire	190	First Boston
06/19	GMAC	755	First Boston
07/23	Chrysler	250	Salomon
07/24	Nissan	188	First Boston
08/19	GMAC	1,080	First Boston
10/14	ABSC	4,000	First Boston
11/13	Western Financial	192	Drexel
11/18	Banco Central	66	First Boston
11/18	GMAC	327	First Boston
12/02	ABSC	180	First Boston
12/05	Goldome	206	First Boston
12/12	Bank of America	514	Salomon
12/17	GMAC	445	First Boston
12/17	Sperry	175	First Boston
	Total	$10,041	
1987			
01/16	RepublicBank	$ 200	Goldman
02/25	Bank of America	400	First Boston
	Total	$ 600	
	Grand Total	$11,877	

Source: First Boston Corporation

an instantaneous change in the interest-rate environment, either up or down 100, 300, or 500 basis points. The CMO, for example, suffers severe negative convexity—that is, negative returns from an interest-rate increase exceeds positive returns from a rate decrease. If interest rates go up 500 basis points, the CMO has a negative return of 14.81 percent, but if interest rates drop 500 basis points, the return is only positive 3.28 percent. That is not a very good trade-off. On the other hand, the corporate debenture experiences a slight positive convexity. The trade-off is 8.34 percent compared to -7.55 percent. All corporate debt securities have slight positive convexity, because there is no prepayment risk. The first GMAC grantor trust also has slight positive convexity, though it is not quite as positive as the corporate debenture.

Table 4 shows a comparison of yield premia for a two-year GMAC, a first tranche two-year CMO, and a GMAC 1985A grantor trust with an average life of approximately two years. The two-year GMAC yields 45 basis points over the Treasury rate compared to the CMO's 95 basis point premium, whereas the GMAC grantor trust has a 75 basis point premium. I would argue that the grantor trust should yield less than the corporate debenture: because of the credit quality of these assets and their prepayment consistency, the 75 basis point premium should be closer to 45 basis points. The principal reason they do not, however, is that people do not understand the asset-backed security yet.

The last two items shown in this table are the $4 billion Asset Backed Securities Corporation Class 1–B ABO, which was structured differently and therefore has lower yields, and finally the credit card issue for Bank of America, which was trading recently at 70 basis points over the Treasury rate.

Finally, Table 5 lists all of the asset-backed issues through March 1987. The volume of the market for 1985 was $1.2 billion. There were seven issues in 1985: the Sperry issue was backed by computer leases; Valley National and Marine Midland issues were backed by automobile loans; and GMAC and Western Financial issues by automobiles. In 1986, there were several more issues, particularly in the second half, for a total of $10 billion. In early 1987, there were two issues backed by credit cards, which had never been done before. These two issues bring the total of the asset-backed securities floated through the first quarter of 1987 to $11.9 billion.

Overall, the development of the primary and secondary markets for asset-backed securities over the past two years has been quite rapid. There have been 28 public issues, of which 19 are pass-throughs, 7 are pay-throughs, and 2 are asset-backed obligations. There are 13 different issuers, and three different types of collateral: automobiles and light trucks, computer leases, and credit cards. With just 2 percent of the $595 billion of consumer installment debt securitized, however, the market still may be considered to be in its infancy. The remainder of 1987 should be characterized by increased activity in asset-backed securities, including the entrance of several first-time issuers as well as repeat issuers; and although most transactions will continue to be collateralized by automobile loans and credit cards, further diversity in the types of assets securitized may be expected.

Question and Answer Session

QUESTION: The evidence supporting indexed bond funds is based on statistics from the bull market of the past five years. How would indexed bond funds look in the previous five years?

NELSON: Actually, over the past 10 years, bond index fund performance looks relatively good versus active manager performance. By that I mean above the median. There is the problem of survival bias with longer time periods, however. For example, on the equity side, there may have been 1000 managers in the immediate past two years, but only 100 managers 10 years ago.

QUESTION: Do you think that home equity loans will become securitized, and if so, what quality do you think they would be?

DUB: Certain home equity loans are virtually identical to what is already being securitized, i.e., automobiles and credit cards, and so I think it is only a question of time before people take the same technology and apply it to home equity loans. It certainly is possible. It is too early to tell what the credit quality would be, but I assume it might be slightly worse than existing asset-based securities because of the greater competition right now to issue home equity loans.

QUESTION: What has been the tracking error with bond index funds? What do you consider a good level?

NELSON: The tracking error on a government bond index fund is probably within 10 to 15 basis points annually. The spread on government corporate index funds increases to 30 to 40 basis points, depending on how many bonds there are in the universe. It is amazing how closely you can track a 5000 bond universe with 100 bonds.

Globalization of Financial Markets: Trends and Implications for Investment Strategy

Michael S. Ivanovitch

The recent surge in the volume of transborder money and capital market operations has led many observers to conclude that the world is witnessing the advent of an entirely new phenomenon in the financial services industry. Yet the process itself is anything but new. European investors, for example, were very much interested in the shares of U.S. mining companies that were actively traded on the Paris Stock Exchange in the late 1890s. Arbitrage transactions involving New York and European equity markets also were quite important throughout the 1930s. In the postwar period, to follow the overseas development of the corporate clients banks began to expand their international activities. In the late 1950s, tax and regulatory arbitrage launched the beginning of vigorous growth in Euromarket financing. The pace of global portfolio diversification has quickened considerably in the past six years, and all major segments of financial markets have become more integrated internationally.

The United States is by far the most prominent participant in this fast-growing international portfolio diversification. Overseas investments of American pension funds grew from less than $1 billion in 1981 to almost $40 billion in 1986. Similar developments have been observed in other countries. For example, the share of foreign security holdings in the portfolios of British pension funds increased from 5 percent in 1978 to 15 percent in 1986; and international assets held by Japanese institutional investors increased to about 15 percent of the total in early 1987, compared with well under 10 percent in 1985.

International portfolios of U.S., Japanese, and U.K. pension funds are estimated to have expanded two to three times as fast as their domestic investments during the period from 1981 to 1986. Total pension fund investments overseas are believed to have reached $80 billion in 1986, nearly double the amount recorded in 1983. Some industry observers expect that by the early 1990s, about $300 billion—or 8 percent of the total pension fund assets—will be invested internationally.

The process of global portfolio diversification is reflected in the increasingly important role played by foreign investors in the major financial markets throughout the world. It is estimated that foreign investors account for more than 50 percent of the total trading volume at the Frankfurt Stock Exchange, nearly 25 percent at the Paris Bourse, and approximately 10 percent at the New York Stock Exchange. Between 1985 and 1986, the total volume of foreign investments on the Madrid Stock Exchange increased more than fivefold, representing 37 percent of the effective turnover in share trading last year.

As mentioned earlier, global financial operations were especially prominent in the field of banking in the late 1950s and 1960s, as banks followed their corporate customers overseas to finance trade and investment transactions. Gradually, however, other market segments also became more global in scope. From very modest beginnings in the late 1950s, Eurocurrency markets eventually developed into a huge and fast-growing pool of financial resources. The volume of Eurobond issues grew sixfold between 1981 and 1986, while the total amount of Euroequities rose from $1 billion in 1984 to $11 billion in 1986, with the shares of about 470 companies now being traded on more than one stock exchange.

Currency trading also has become an important global market, with daily volume of some $200 billion being transacted in London, New York, Tokyo, and Zurich.

FACTORS INFLUENCING THE PROCESS OF GLOBALIZATION

A complex interaction of public policies, markets, and technological advances has been the main force behind the internationalization of financial transactions. The most important policy measures have been the elimination of capital controls and the granting of permission to foreign financial institutions to operate in what formerly were closed and heavily-protected domestic financial markets. Large budget deficits observed in most industrial countries in the past two decades also have played a major role in the development of both domestic and international bond markets. In some countries, specific policy actions have been designed to promote the international competitive position of large financial centers. To attract and retain jobs and income created by the financial industry, these governments have offered more liberal access to their financial markets and have allowed residents to tap lending and investment resources abroad.

This greater freedom to operate abroad has given further impetus to the process of financial innovation. New financial assets and techniques have been designed to widen the choice of investment and borrowing outlets, lower intermediation costs, enhance liquidity, and provide effective tools of risk management. These developments have brought various financial systems around the globe closer together. Interest rate and currency swaps are particularly good examples. In addition, a host of procedures has evolved to make it possible to unbundle risks, and then price and sell them separately.

The growing investor sophistication and the constant search for balanced, hedged, and less volatile portfolios have been important to the globalization process. Increasingly, the acquisition of foreign assets has been viewed as a way of achieving these objectives while escaping the limitations of narrow domestic financial markets. This process has been aided by the strong bull market experienced by a large number of stock exchanges.

In addition to public policy measures and spontaneous market developments, advances in technology and telecommunications have played an important role as well. The fact that information can be processed and disseminated at a lower cost and with greater speed and accuracy has improved the overall market efficiency through more competitive pricing, market making, and settlement procedures.

All of these factors will continue to operate in the foreseeable future, forcing an ever-increasing degree of integration of financial debtors around the globe. A further liberalization of financial transactions, screen-based trading, and better research will make portfolio diversification one of the main driving forces of this process. At the same time, important regional integration initiatives, such as the one planned by the EEC for 1992, will create huge and homogeneous markets for a vast array of financial services.

On the supply side, the pool of investment outlets will continue to grow, in part because of large privatization programs in the industrialized countries and debt-equity conversions in the developing world. The Paris Stock Exchange, for example, plans to increase its capitalization by FF 200 billion by 1990 through privatization-related share offerings. This rising volume of equities will have to be traded internationally because many domestic markets remain too thin and narrow to be able to absorb these new issues in an orderly fashion.

Similarly, the strong growth momentum of asset demand observed in the past few years should continue in the future. Mutual funds have attracted an increasing number of small savers to the stock and bond markets, and the demographic developments in several countries have led to an exceptionally fast growth of pension funds and various individual retirement arrangements. In Japan, for example, pension fund resources in the past 10 years have grown at a compound annual rate of 23 percent to the total of 20 trillion yen in 1986.

These developments suggest that globalization of financial transactions is a deeply rooted and irreversible process rather than a passing fad, as some observers thought a few years ago. U.S. investment managers are not likely to ignore 52 percent of world equities and $2.4 trillion of stock market capital existing outside the United States.

THE OUTLOOK FOR ECONOMIC ACTIVITY AND CREDIT MARKETS

United States

There is not likely to be a recession in the United States this year or next; nor will there be vigorous economic conditions. Most likely, the economy will be edging along a 2 percent growth path for the rest of this year and perhaps slightly above that in 1988, assuming that there is a significant improvement in the economic condition of the other major industrial nations. The inflation rate should be between 5 and 6 percent by the end of the year, and the dollar should continue to move lower in a relatively orderly fashion to compensate for the lack of progress in the international adjustment of demand management policies. The weakening dollar and reviving inflationary pressures will preclude any appreciable easing of credit market conditions, despite the fact that softening aggregate demand would require lower, rather than higher, interest rates. Only a distinct turnaround in trade performance, coupled with easier credit conditions abroad, would make it possible to stem large capital outflows from dollar assets and, eventually, to reduce interest rates in the United States.

Japan

The Japanese economy has been advancing at an unusually slow pace in the past two years. Deteriorating net exports, in volume terms, have further aggravated the situation in the most recent period, and it now seems likely that the economy may grow less than 2.5 percent in 1987. Consumer spending should remain weak as a result of record low wage settlements, falling bonus payments, and steadily worsening labor market conditions. Business capital outlays also have decelerated substantially, particularly in the manufacturing sector. Residential construction, on the other hand, is the only component of aggregate demand enjoying exceptionally strong growth as a result of fiscal incentives and declining mortgage costs.

It is doubtful, though, whether housing by itself can generate sufficient growth momentum in the absence of a significant increase in public expenditures. Apart from the usual front-end loading, there is nothing to suggest that the Japanese government is prepared to step up its spending programs in the first part of the fiscal 1987–1988. The progressive weakening of the economy might lead to a supplementary budget later this year, but once again, this will probably turn out to be too little and too late. Thus, it seems likely that excess liquidity, weak credit

demand, and strengthening currency should continue to exert downward pressure on the Japanese interest rates over the next few quarters.

Germany

The situation prevailing in Germany is fairly similar, except that consumption spending remains slightly stronger and the trade balance has not deteriorated nearly as much, in volume terms, because of a more diversified export activity. Economic growth in Germany this year could end up below 2 percent, which is less than the original government forecast of 2.5 percent. Factory orders, industrial production, construction, and business investment all remain rather weak and are likely to worsen as a result of declining international competitiveness and softening external demand. Yet there is practically no chance, at this juncture, that present fiscal policies might become more expansionary to offset the growing weakness of final demand in the private sector.

The decelerating economic activity, rising exchange rate and persisting deflationary pressures should lead to markedly lower interest rates in Germany for the rest of this year. This is likely to provide more room for similar interest-rate movements in other countries of the European Monetary System (EMS), where inflation and current account performance remain favorable.

United Kingdom

The United Kingdom is the only major industrial economy where growth conditions over the near term look relatively good. Consumption spending continues to advance rapidly as a result of strong disposable income gains.

Export activity also appears to have picked up considerably, spurred by the sterling's decline vis-a-vis the European Monetary System bloc. The outlook beyond the next few quarters is quite uncertain, however, because of the substantial risks posed by the buoyant domestic demand and credit growth for current account and inflation.

IMPLICATIONS FOR INVESTMENT STRATEGY

The picture emerging for economic activity in major industrial countries is one of slow growth, declining credit demand, and generally subdued inflationary pressures. The persistence of large financial imbalances calls for significant policy shifts, with fiscal contraction in the United States and both monetary and fiscal expansion in countries where current account surpluses, low inflation, and weak demand conditions continue to prevail. Such an adjustment would facilitate an orderly realignment of exchange rates without putting undue pressures on currency movements and creating too much volatility in financial markets.

Experience thus far indicates that these policy changes will be slow and insufficient, implying that markets will have to compensate for the lack of policy action by forcing adjustments through an exchange-rate-induced impact on economic activity and total asset returns. This means that the dollar will continue to decline until there is convincing evidence of a decisive turnaround in U.S. trade accounts and until the fiscal/monetary mix in major surplus countries becomes more expansionary.

The expected easing of credit conditions outside the United States bodes well for foreign bond markets. By contrast, equities abroad may be more treacherous because of slower growth and falling corporate profits in the export-oriented sectors. This does not mean that share prices in major industrial countries will not be rising. Lower interest rates, portfolio diversification, and movement out of dollar-denominated instruments may promote share ownership. Whereas, these equity markets will continue to offer attractive investment possibilities, it is important to bear in mind that most of them still remain relatively thin, and that share prices in a number of cases have been run up due to regulatory changes (such as the formation of mutual funds, allowing pension funds to invest in equities, or the holding of equities as part of tax-free individual retirement programs) rather than any major shifts in the outlook for economic growth and corporate earnings.

Specific institutional and regulatory features, and the differing positions of overseas markets within the international business cycle will therefore make good, timely, and comprehensive research more important than ever for a successful international investment strategy.

Question and Answer Session

QUESTION: What do you consider a dangerous level for the dollar versus the DM and the yen?

IVANOVITCH: The dangerous level of an exchange rate is very difficult to define. Whoever asked that question might find comfort in being reminded that the finance ministers who met in Paris in late February, 1987, thought the current dollar-yen and dollar-DM rates were just about adequate in terms of the underlying economic relationships. Personally, I would define the danger level in terms of inflation potential and large outflows from dollar assets.

Devaluation-induced upward pressures on costs and prices in our country are not as powerful as they are in smaller, open economies where imports represent between 25 and 40 percent of GNP. Nevertheless, they are very important, as we are beginning to see in our price indexes. But that is not the whole story. In addition to higher prices of imported goods and services, there also are the so-called sympathetic price increases, when our import-competing industries—which have been straightjacketed by foreign competition since 1981—all of a sudden begin to raise their prices in response to the falling dollar and rising prices of their foreign competitors. This is an extremely dangerous phenomenon that often is neglected in much of the analysis dealing with the inflationary impact of a devaluing currency.

The answer with regard to portfolio implications is much more difficult. Technically, of course, the danger level depends on the expected total returns on dollar assets versus those denominated in other currencies. In terms of fixed-income instruments, the two crucial variables are the interest-rate differentials and expected currency rates, assuming there are not important fiscal distortions. Clearly, if the currency losses are not offset by capital gains arising from yield differentials, there will be a withdrawal from dollar investments. If our earlier scenario works in the sense of lower interest rates in Japan and Germany, there need not be a dangerous outflow from U.S. assets, and the prospects for more stable exchange-rate rela-

tionships would be that much greater. Similarly, relatively low equity prices in the United States, along with the breadth and liquidity of our stock exchanges, represent important advantages that many foreign investors weigh carefully before taking their funds elsewhere.

QUESTION: Why should U.S. unions permit their pension funds to invest abroad and improve the productivity of non-U.S. workers?

IVANOVITCH: The answer is simple—they would do that in order to realize returns greater than those available at home.

QUESTION: Would not the full benefit of globalization require an increase in foreign direct investment in pace with portfolio investment?

IVANOVITCH: As a rule, the two go pari passu, because capital outflows are just the mirror image of current account surpluses. The growing importance of Japan, Germany and, to a lesser extent, the United Kingdom as providers of direct and portfolio investments are the most obvious examples of that phenomenon. Although these two kinds of capital flows respond to different sets of determining factors, it is true that both of them seek to exploit the possibilities for investment returns that are higher than those in the country of origin. In that sense, they contribute to the process of globalization of financial markets.

QUESTION: Is there such a thing as a French Treasury bond with a coupon? How different is it from a U.S. Treasury bond?

IVANOVITCH: Yes, there is. These bonds are at times patterned on some of the innovations in our Treasury bond markets and could be quite similar to the ones available here. The basic features offered by French government bonds consist of fixed and floating-rate tranches, with the possibility of switching tranches a year or two from the date of issue.

Innovative Securities and the International Debt Crisis

Paul A. Volcker

Though the Federal Reserve does not have an institutional view of innovative securities, I do worry about them. I worry about how the use of innovative securities impacts the stability of the entire financial system. The international debt situation is a good example of some of the potential problems in this area.

INNOVATIVE SECURITIES: SOME CONCERNS

Most of the new innovative securities could not have existed years ago. It is now possible to unpackage risk and repackage it in other ways, enabling people to get on their appropriate indifference curve. The question should be raised, however, as to how carefully that is done. Is there an appreciation of the systemic risks that do continue? Are there risks actually aggravated by some of these new instruments? The world cannot be hedged. There is no way to eliminate the risks arising from real changes in the economy, real business fluctuations, and real inflation. They can be redistributed, perhaps, to those who are willing to bear those risks, but the risks are still there.

Will some of the systemic problems be eased or aggravated by innovative securities? The speed with which these instruments can be used is of concern. People hedge, for example, by going into futures or options markets. In the ordinary performance of the market, these instruments are indeed insurance policies. But what happens when events occur that trigger systemic problems in unaccustomed volume with unaccustomed speed? One must consider the unresolved question of the impact of triple witching hours on the stock market. I do not think the phenomenon has been occurring long enough to say whether the systemic risks have been tested. Without more experience in adverse circumstances, however, caution is important.

Most of these new instruments have very legitimate purposes and are useful as part of legitimate investment strategies; however, they also are a temptation to speculate in greater volume. They make speculation easier and cheaper than in the past. Again, that is a question of what systemic problems may be aggravated when everybody tries to get through the gate together in adverse market circumstances.

Some of these new instruments do not seem all that new. There is much talk about mortgage-backed securities these days, but there were mortgage bonds in the 1920s that looked a great deal like mortgage-backed securities. The ultimate experience of those securities was not happy.

INTERNATIONAL DEBT

When I began work in the field of economics, it was taken as an article of faith that international lending was much better if it was done in the banking system rather than in the securities markets. There had been a lot of international lending done in the securities markets, both in developing countries and in industrialized countries. When those loans went bad, they went bad with a vengeance. The situation could not be managed very easily when the ownership of the securities was diverse. There was no common interest, no common negotiating point to bring them together, and there was a fairly rapid collapse of the international credit system.

Many economists, looking back at that experience, said that we should never again get involved in that type of lending. International lending should be done through the banking system, where the risks can then be managed, renegotiated, and dealt with more easily should difficulties arise. The real lesson of that experience was: do not do that volume of international lending at all. We are violating that stricture now, but it is done largely through the banking system. We tend to go the full cycle in this thinking, however. There is much discussion now suggesting that we would be much better off if all the international loans were turned into securities, the argument being that individuals can take the losses; they would not be concentrated in a few banking organizations, thus jeopardizing the whole system.

Although there are no final truths in this area, I will defend the proposition that we are fortunate, given the size of the international debts, that they are concentrated in the banking system, and that the laborious case-by-case process of negotiation that has been going on has achieved something. There has been some degree of success, and this does provide the most promising scenario, however much criticized these days, for dealing with this important problem over the next few years.

THE BANKING SYSTEM'S EXPOSURE

The exposure of the lending institutions themselves has not changed much in absolute terms when one contrasts the present situation with 1982, when the crisis became overt. Relative to the capital of the lending banks and their assets, particularly relative to their capital, which has been growing faster than their assets, the problem is only half as great—probably less than that worldwide. It is almost exactly half as great for American banks. The relative exposure has probably declined more than 50 percent for foreign banks, because most of these loans are in dollars and their main balance sheet is in other currencies, and the dollar has been depreciating. That is important in evaluating the systemic risk that remains in this general area. If all of those loans went bad, it is still only half as bad as it would have been in 1982 in terms of jeopardizing the banking system. Without minimizing the problem that remains—if all the loans went bad today, it would be a very big problem—it is more manageable than it was four or five years ago. If that kind of improvement is projected over the next three to four years, you begin to have a debt situation that, in terms of its impact on the world economy and the world financial system, has passed a real crisis point. The crisis has not been managed completely, but I would argue that we are a good part of the way there.

THE BORROWER'S PERSPECTIVE

Looking at it from the standpoint of the borrowers, which is perhaps more important in terms of immediate welfare, there are some signs of progress in terms of reduction of the debt burden. It is not as clear country by country, because specific countries like Mexico and Ecuador have been affected by declines in oil prices and natural disasters. If you look at the debt relative to income or exports for an oil exporter, it looks slightly worse today than it would have four years ago. But if you look at other countries, by and large the debt burden has declined relative to their capacity to service the debt. At the same time in recent years—again with some exceptions—those countries have begun to grow again. The decline in their standard of living, which is a very real outgrowth of the debt crisis, has been stemmed, and is beginning to improve again.

Many of the countries with large debt problems have undertaken economic policy measures of a kind that are basically favorable for the long run. In good part because they were under debt pressures, they felt the need to change economic policies in a constructive direction. I would define a constructive direction as a generally more liberal, outward-looking direction with less state domination. They are freer in trade, they are less subsidized internally, and they have somewhat smaller governmental sectors relative to the rest of the economy.

Is the change terribly dramatic? In most countries, no. Is it very even? Are they making steady progress year after year? Generally it is more like three steps forward and two steps backward. But, they are making more progress than they made at any time in the previous post-war period, when most of them were moving toward closed economies, state control, more subsidies, and more import barriers. I see a clear change in the direction of economic policy in a more promising direction.

Although I will not claim that everything has gone perfectly, I am inclined to argue that the debt has been reasonably well managed, both from the standpoint of the borrower and the creditors. This is largely because it was relatively concentrated in the hands of institutional lenders that could discuss their common interests. In recent months, the sense of common interest and overriding common need that is essential to solving the problem has greatly diminished. The centrifugal forces among both the borrowers and the lenders have been increasing. The sense of frustration has been increasing, in part because there is less sense of crisis. This places the success of the whole effort in jeopardy.

From that perspective, consider the situation in Brazil, where the government ran into a severe internal economic problem and suspended interest payments, most of them to private creditors. By conveying a new sense of crisis, that action may provide an impetus for a renewed and more constructive effort toward dealing with the remaining problems in other countries and eventually in Brazil itself. Alternatively, it has caused some discussion on whether the whole strategy ought to be changed and abandoned. The choice is between approaching this problem with renewed vigor, and building upon what I think is a very substantial measure of success, or determining that the divisive and centrifugal forces among both the creditors and borrowers will overcome the effort. I think the system as a whole—as well as individual institutions—is enough exposed so that the risk of the effort not proceeding is very substantial. Therefore, as you think about all those new instruments and how you can use them, there are some very basic problems regarding the use and abuse of credit in the modern financial system; the international debt situation is simply one.

Question and Answer Session

QUESTION: Have you enjoyed being chairman of the Federal Reserve Board enough to be interested in serving for a few more years?

VOLCKER: My job is not one where I get up in the morning and say: "Gee, it's another day full of fun and games; I want to get into the office early." While there is a certain sense of challenge about it when you get all finished, fun is not the word I use to describe being chairman of the Federal Reserve Board.

QUESTION: If you were to be appointed chairman in 1987, would you like to be known in later years as a great deflation fighter, as the defender of the American dollar, or as the great inflation fighter?

VOLCKER: I would like to be known as the great proponent of stability and growth. When I was appointed chairman in 1979, I wondered how I would measure whether I was successful in the job. What would be the measure of success for the head of a central bank, or the chairman of the Federal Reserve Board? I thought to myself, back in August 1979, that if you had to take one single measure of success, perhaps it was the international value of the dollar. By 1983, however, I had overcome that particular measure of success.

QUESTION: What is your primary concern over the next year regarding the domestic economy: renewed inflation, unemployment, or recession? Is there an acceptable long-term rate of inflation?

VOLCKER: I do not think there is an acceptable inflation rate. The economy is going to operate better with some sense of continuing stability, and people are not calculating their investment performance, either financial investment or real investment, on the basis of what they fear or hope about major changes in the price level. We are a long way from the place where some reasonable degree of price stability is taken for granted. So long as that is the case, there will not be optimum economic performance, partly because interest rates hang, all other things equal, higher than they otherwise would be.

The risks for the economy in the year ahead are substantial. The great achievement of the past four or five years has been that we have managed, for the first time in years, to combine a fairly long period of business expansion with progress toward price stability. By the end of 1986, partly because of oil prices, the rate of inflation was less than at the beginning of the expansion. That is rather unusual after four years of expansion. It was not a fluke; it probably would have been lower in 1986 than in 1985 even without the oil situation, because the basic wage trends and productivity trends in manufacturing were pretty good. That is the good side.

The obvious risk to the economy is represented by those two big, not unrelated, deficits—the budget deficit and the trade deficit. I think there is some cause and effect between the budget deficit and the trade deficit. It is very hard to see how we could finance our budget deficit these days without a big inflow of capital from abroad, and you cannot have big inflows of capital from abroad without running a big current account deficit. That is what we are doing, and so far capital has come in pretty easily. But, will that capital continue so freely as our external debt builds up? And if it does not, what are the implications for financial markets, for interest rates, for the exchange rate and, therefore, for inflation? That is the risk that keeps me awake at night.

The risks of the American economy arise, in part, from sluggish growth abroad. I would not worry about the risks, particularly in terms of the rate of growth, if we were operating in a stronger world environment. The European growth rate, however, has not been very rapid in recent years and, except in the United Kingdom, it seems to be slowing rather than rising. Most forecasts for Europe project growth rates significantly below 2 percent in countries that have high levels of unemployment. That goes for Japan, too. The developing countries do not provide opportunities for the United States to have striking improvements in our external position, but we are counting on improvements in our external position to carry the economy along at a modest rate of speed. In particular, improvement in our current account is important, both for its own sake and because of its implications for carrying U.S. economic activity forward. I do not think it is of crucial importance that we have a great boom in the United States after four years of expansion, but I think a certain amount of forward momentum is important.

QUESTION: How important is money supply growth? Does it make sense to follow money supply growth targets? Are there other indicators of growth, inflation, or economic activity that are more significant? Do you think that the recent growth in M1 is being reflected in the rapid rise in stock prices this year?

VOLCKER: There are many questions about the nature of the relationship among the various measures of money supply, economic activity, and inflation. There is no doubt that a relationship between money and inflation exists. Identifying that relationship, at this particular time, given the rapid institutional changes and the sizeable increases in interest rates over the past 18 months, is very difficult. I would never have anticipated, going into 1986, that M1 was going to increase by 15 or 16 percent, or that the economy would have grown by 2 percent and the inflation rate would be less than 2 percent. That combination of circumstances would not have occurred to me as the most plausible set of forecasts for 1986.

Now that the broader monetary aggregates are behaving more normally, there is much less velocity in M2 and M3. Although velocity did decline in 1986, it was not so clearly out of line with historical experience, and was in the same direction as M1. The M1–GNP relationship is pretty much outside the range of historical experience, except for wars and great depressions, neither of which we have at the moment.

I do think that the rate of growth in money, given the circumstances that prevailed in 1986 and early 1987, helped fuel a general exuberance in financial markets. The financial markets would not have been quite as exuberant with less money creation, all other things being equal. And that worries me.

The stock market did not worry me very much in 1986, but there has been a very rapid rate of debt creation. Historically, one of the more stable relationships has been the level of total net non-financial debt relative to GNP. This has held at about 1.4 for the whole post war period, and it was quite stable in the earlier period as well. In the recent four-year period, however, the debt/GNP ratio has gone from 1.4 to 1.8, an increase of almost 30 percent.

What does this say about the leverage of America and our vulnerablity to the inevitable future economic adversity? That is a legitimate concern facing virtually every sector of the economy. Obviously, the government debt has helped to push up the debt ratio, but so has corporate debt, consumer debt, and mortgage debt. This economic phenomenon is carrying the entire economy into an area that it has never been before. I am not reassured by people who remind me that it is still higher in Japan. That may be so, but it has not been higher in the United States before, and I worry about the consequences, and the extent to which monetary policy may have facilitated that. On the other hand, given the relatively sluggish economy and the improved inflation rate over the past 18 months, it is hard to conclude that we should have been appreciably tighter. Regardless, the debt situation is cause for concern.

QUESTION: Countless solutions have been offered on the management of the debt, ranging from suggesting that the Japanese support a separate entity to hold the defaulted loans of all banks, funded in part by the government, to suggesting that the money center banks should put most of their LDC loans on a non-accrual basis. Are we approaching a creditor/debtor crisis in the United States that will require some sort of a sweeping solution, either by the central bank or by the banks themselves?

VOLCKER: We do not need to face that crisis if both the creditors and the debtors follow what is in their basic self-interest, as they have been doing in the past four years. It cannot be taken for granted, but I do think we need not have that crisis.

I think there has been some misunderstanding about this Japanese "initiative". This arose essentially because the Japanese banks were facing the same problems U.S. banks faced—

they could not reserve against their LDC exposure, or write it down, and get any tax advantages out of the process. The Japanese tax authorities, as all tax authorities, have not been forthcoming about permitting tax deductions for reserving against these debts. There are pretty tough rules concerning when a bank gets a write-off on a bad loan.

The Japanese banks are sitting on sizeable stock portfolios in which there is a great deal of unrealized appreciation. Someone thought up the idea of setting up a corporation in the Cayman Islands for tax reasons. The banks would then park some of the loans over there, take a writedown on them, and since a transaction occurred, the Finance Ministry would allow the liquidation of a certain amount of their stock in portfolio. They would not have to pay taxes on the liquidation of their appreciated securities, but could effectively wash it off against the loss on the loans. My understanding is that it will be limited to a relatively small percentage of those loans.

This scheme has stimulated discussion in Washington of setting up that kind of facility on an international basis with one significant difference. The Japanese arrangement does not relieve the debtor of the ultimate obligation, so it is not a relief to the borrowing country. But the idea circulating in Washington is to establish some kind of international facility, put the loans in the facility, determine a writedown, perhaps related to market values, and writedown the loans on bank balance sheets. In addition, the loan would be entirely or partially forgiven, thus providing some debt relief. I cannot see how a facility of that sort would work without some type of a public guarantee of the entity that takes the loans.

Otherwise, the writedowns would become much larger than anyone is envisioning now, and you would not get the debt relief for the borrower. It violates the underlying assumption that the developed countries, the industrial countries, are not willing to appropriate public monies in any important way. They may do it indirectly through the World Bank, but they would not support directly what would appear to be a bail-out for the banks. And this would be a kind of negotiated partial bail-out. This is one of the objections I have to the approach.

QUESTION: What would the central bank's position be regarding the ultimate securitization of farm loan packages?

VOLCKER: Some securitization of those loans would be resisted given the problem that exists. I am glad that these loans were not all securitized when we started, because then we would have had an even bigger crisis. But securitization may be helpful as a way of gradually working out of some of the problems. I would not see that happening on such a scale that it accounts for breaking the back of the problem, however.

QUESTION: Do you believe in the idea of an economic long cycle? And, if so, do you think economic long waves are inevitable, or can they be put off?

VOLCKER: It is tempting to conclude from history that there have been some long waves. Although I do not know how predictable they are, I suspect they can be changed by human intervention. I do not overestimate the powers of human intervention, however, over any period of time. I think there are some economic forces that tend to go beyond governments, and sometimes governments aggravate the underlying problem. The predictability of that is close to nil in terms of the time horizon that financial people are worried about, which I expect, at the longest, goes to the end of next quarter.

QUESTION: On taxes, you have emphasized in Congressional hearings many times that it is important to look not only at the growth side, but also at the cost-saving side. You have also said that you lose very little sleep over the likelihood of Congress not spending too much, or not saving enough money. In the latest tax reform, the tax legislation has come a long way towards changing that structure. Do you think there is a possibility of tax increases either in the personal structure, the corporate structure, or in the oil tax area?

VOLCKER: I think the chances are better than 50–50 that there will be some revenue increases enacted this year, but I do not think it will be in the form of an income tax or an oil import fee. The most likely areas are cigarettes, cigars, and gasoline. I do not think it is going to be an enormous increase. If there is not a revenue ingredient, there will not be a meaningful deficit-reduction package. The forces will be so divisive that they will never agree on defense spending; they will never agree on civilian spending; they will never agree on taxes; they will agree on nothing. That is my political judgment.

QUESTION: What is the Federal Reserve Board doing with respect to monetary policy?

VOLCKER: We are not doing anything that can be isolated as a magic key. We must look at a variety of factors; for example, how the inflation rate is affected by a rise from the recovery in the oil price and the import prices. If that seems to be setting off a more cumulative movement, then we look at commodity prices as an indicator of a more generalized inflationary phenomenon. We look at the dollar under current circumstances—and my point of view is: Enough is enough in terms of depreciation of the dollar. We also look at the economic momentum, and at all the monetary aggregates. That should yield a fairly easy answer if they all tend to give the same answer.

The problem arises when some factors indicate a need to tighten and some a need to ease up, and then it comes down to a matter of judgment. That is where we are currently. I think it is the only sensible approach to take, given the breakdown of some of the relationships that we thought we could rely on more fully, particularly between money and the economy. Few of us have much confidence in those kinds of monetary relationships today. That may change two years from now. Today, major monetary policy moves cannot be made simply on the basis of one, two, or even three months, or on any single monetary number. There should be some confirming or contradictory evidence before a decision to move is made. That complicates policy-making, and is not conducive to a high level of confidence, because people would like to feel that policymakers are constrained by something that may be measured. That is not the way of the world in 1987.

QUESTION: Could the weakness in the FSLIC, the Federal Farm Credit problem, or the Pension Benefit Guarantee Corporation financial situa-

tion be potential triggers to a crisis of confidence?

VOLCKER: They could. I worry less about the pension problem, because it does not have the same confidence and liquidity implications for the general public. Everyone has been too blase about these kinds of problems. There is a general assumption in the marketplace that the government or the Federal Reserve Board will take care of everything. I think that is a gross overestimation of the ultimate capacity of the government or the Federal Reserve Board. It gives rise to certain types of unhealthy behavior. People do not worry about the FSLIC, or the FDIC, or the Farm Credit, because the government is going to take care of it.

Obviously the government is concerned about the FSLIC, and I think the government has a commitment to take care of the FSLIC; but it needs to be done in a way that is most conducive to long-term stability. The fact that so many people continue to deposit in savings and loans that have negative net worths is an unhealthy situation. It is not only unhealthy for financial markets ultimately, because those institutions will bid up rates for everybody, but it is very corrosive in terms fundamental financial disciplines. In the short run, the government will have to take care of the FSLIC, and protect that situation; but in the long run, the system must be reexamined. It must be made clear that self-reliance is not absent from the system, as I am afraid has become the case of the S&L business and to some degree the banking business.

QUESTION: There has been a great deal of debate over the issue of deregulation. The Federal Reserve Board has had a very serious and stable position on deregulation of financial institutions. Would you comment on whether or not some deregulation or strengthening of the financial industry through the industrial sector might be appropriate?

VOLCKER: You cannot approach the question simply as a matter of whether in a specific instance the acquisition of banks or savings and loans by commercial firms might strengthen the system as a whole, or certainly those particular institutions, though that might well be the case when the system is in difficulty. You have to consider the question of what is the best structure over time, both from the standpoint of safety and soundness of the system, and from the standpoint of other basic considerations about the concentration of economic power and conflicts of interest. I would argue that the fact that the banking and savings and loan systems are guaranteed by the government, adds considerable weight to that view. That guarantee, however, also gives rise to certain behavior by managers of banks and savings and loans which must then be dealt with through regulation. Risk is curtailed by supervision, rather than by normal market incentives.

Should we have an economic system where commercial and industrial firms, as well as banks and savings and loans, can hide behind that same so-called federal safety net? These institutions will either benefit from the safety net, or it will have to be abandoned. Who is brave enough to propose that we run a modern economy without a safety net comprising the Federal Reserve, the FDIC, and so forth? Yet having it implies a certain amount of regulation. We do not want to regulate the likes of Sears-Roebuck, but if we do not, we run the risk that they will use the mantle of an insured institution subject to liquidity support and other governmental protection to support other activities. One solution that has been proposed is to insulate the bank from the rest of the company. I think that goes contrary to human nature. Not only is it difficult to insulate one part of a company from the rest, but if you were so draconian as to do that, then any economic reason for combining the two in the first place disappears. Sears-Roebuck management does not want to run a bank as an isolated institution; nor does American Express.

Why are such companies so eager to have a bank when banks want to get out of the banking business? They want to be able to leverage themselves like the bank. And why can a bank leverage itself so much? Because it is a federally-protected institution. You may argue about the degree of protection, but it is protected. Banks can leverage themselves 20 to 1, but do we want all industries leveraged 20 to 1? The answer to that is self-evident: we do not. If we do not want to regulate them all, we had better separate them. This overlaps with the issue of whether financial institutions should feel their first responsibility is to the customers, to the parent itself, or to the customers of the parent, when it comes to lending money or issuing deposits. There is a strong tendency to have self-dealing among the various parts of the institution and to cross-market services, which does not give the best and most competitive financial system. On that particular issue, we need a lot of changes, but I would preserve separation between banking and commerce.

QUESTION: Please comment on the recent Securities and Exchange Commission (SEC) investigations of the financial community.

VOLCKER: I do not think I have any particular comment. Those things largely involve areas outside my immediate concern. Though we are all concerned with honesty and morality, they are separate from safety and soundness. Yet the temptations that give rise to this kind of behavior are a cautionary note to what could happen to issues affecting safety and soundness in a system that has enormous rewards for certain types of deals. It is basically an unhealthy situation when so much money may be made in such concentrated areas from certain types of deals. It should not be surprising that a lot of corners are cut in doing those deals. Insider trading is one aspect of that. That may not be the part that I worry about for the safety and soundness of the system, but there are activities out there motivated by the same highly-concentrated rewards that are damaging the soundness of the system. I am not happy with the behavior patterns represented by the gross and unhealthy incentives that exist in the marketplace.

Self-Evaluation Examination Questions

Which of these factors have contributed to the explosion of innovations in fixed-income securities and markets:

    I.   The deregulation of the banking and financial system.
    II.   The restructuring of corporate America.
    III. Increased exchange-rate volatility.
    IV. Increased awareness of the importance of world financial markets.
    V.   Increased competition among securities dealers and investment managers.

  a) I, II, and III
  b) I, III, and IV
  c) II, III, and V
  d) All of the above.
  e) None of the above.

2. Savings and loan institutions have benefitted from which of the following financial innovations:
  a) A global market for interest-rate swaps.
  b) Securitization of home mortgages.
  c) Portfolio insurance.
  d) Adjustable-rate mortgages.
  e) The introduction of options on futures.

3. The junk bond market is worth approximately:
  a) $50 billion
  b) $100 billion
  c) $500 billion
  d) $1 trillion
  e) $3 trillion

4. The credit cycle begins and ends with:
  a) Manic optimism.
  b) Manic pessimism.
  c) Skepticism.
  d) Greed.
  e) Fear.

5. The distinction sometimes made between junk bonds and high-yield bonds is that:
  a) Junk bonds are rated below B, while high-yield bonds are rated between Baa (BBB) and B.
  b) Junk bonds have high risks at time of issue, while high-yield bonds are bonds in default.
  c) Junk bonds have no agency ratings, whereas high-yield bonds are rated at below investment grade by the agencies.
  d) Junk bonds are likely to default, while high-yield bonds are not.
  e) Junk bonds are bonds of reasonable quality when issued that have fallen on bad times, while high-yield bonds are initially issued with high levels of risk.

6. High-yield bonds have been characterized by:
  a) High returns, moderate volatility, high defaults.
  b) Moderate returns, high volatility, low defaults.
  c) High returns, low volatility, low defaults.
  d) Moderate returns, moderate volatility, moderate defaults.
  e) low returns, moderate volatility, high defaults

7. When everyone loves high-yield bonds, it will be time to:
   a) Buy.
   b) Hold.
   c) Sell.

8. Ideally, unbundling and rebundling the flows from fixed-rate mortgages provides:
   a) Profits to investment bankers.
   b) More predictable cash flows.
   c) Concentration of the uncertainty about cash flows in ways that are more readily understood.
   d) Reduced uncertainty about defaults.
   e) b and c.

9. The beauty of interest-only and principal-only security strips is:
   a) Their simplicity.
   b) The arbitrage potential in creating them.
   c) The reduction in interest rate risk associated with each of them.
   d) The elimination of prepayment risk compared to the underlying mortgages.
   e) The ability to use them to create a security with virtually any coupon and prepayment characteristics desired.

10. Discount securities can be created by:
    a) Stripping off part of the principal from a high-coupon security.
    b) Stripping off a portion of the coupon from a current coupon security.
    c) Adding coupon to a low coupon security.
    d) Adding coupon to a high coupon security.
    e) Stripping off principal from a low coupon security.

11. CMO equity arises from:
    I.   The arbitrage potential from taking a pool of mortgages and breaking it up into maturity tranches.
    II. Income earned on undistributed funds in the CMO trust.
    III. Overcollateralization of the CMO trust.
    IV. Funds left over when some of the mortgages are prepaid.
    V.   Prepayment penalties on the mortgages.

    a) I and III.
    b) III and V.
    c) I and II.
    d) All of the above.
    e) None of the above.

12. The value of the CMO equity when the collateral is traditional fixed-rate mortgages:
    a) Increases when interest rates rise.
    b) Decreases when interest rates rise.

13. Early asset-linked debt instruments were tied to:
    a) Gold.
    b) Petroleum.
    c) The consumer price index.
    d) Currencies.
    e) Stock market indexes.

14. The most important need asset-linked securities meet is to:
    a) Allow institutions that cannot hold physical assets, futures or options on these assets to establish a position in these assets.
    b) Provide alternative routes for producers to sell the assets.
    c) Create commodities options that are not regulated by the Commodities Futures Trading Commission.
    d) Allow investors to purchase long-dated options that are otherwise not available.
    e) Increase the liquidity of the basic debt security.

15. A problem with asset-linked debt securities is:
    a) Lack of liquidity.
    b) The highly idiosyncratic nature of the individual issues.
    c) Difficulty in valuing the option component.
    d) Difficulty in understanding them.
    e) Potential regulatory problems.

16. The System Dynamics National Model was developed:
    a) By analyzing historical economic trends and cycles.
    b) By applying neo-Keynesian analysis to business behavior.
    c) By combining the best elements of monetarism and supply-side economics.
    d) By applying the theory of the Kondratieff cycle.
    e) By working upward from the corporate level of decision-making to a model of the national economy.

17. According to the National System Dynamics Model as interpreted by Forrester, we are in a period of:
    a) High economic growth.
    b) Economic stability.
    c) Economic decline.

18. Arguments against indexing bond portfolios include:
    I.   It is expensive.
    II. There is no reason to think indexed portfolios of bonds are efficient portfolios.
    III. The results compare poorly with those of active management
    IV. The indexed portfolios may have characteristics, such as changing duration, that are not liked or desired by the investor.
    V.   It provides excessive structure to investing in fixed-income markets.

    a) I and II.
    b) II and III.
    c) II and IV.
    d) All of the above.
    e) None of the above.

19. Two approaches for structuring an indexed portfolio include:
    I.   Stratified sampling.
    II. Dedication.
    III. Immunization.
    IV. Contingent immunization.
    V.   The "risk-model" approach.

    a) II and III.
    b) I and III.
    c) I and IV.
    d) IV and V.
    e) II and IV.

20. Aside from mortgages, the most common asset to be securitized is:
    a) Credit card receivables.
    b) Leases on computers.
    c) Accounts receivable of textile firms .
    d) Inventories.
    e) Installment debt on autos and light trucks.

21. To investors, attractive characteristics of securitized assets include all the following except:
    a) High credit quality.
    b) Familiarity and understanding.
    c) High yields.
    d) Lack of event risk.
    e) Consistent prepayment experience.

22. The volume of securitized asset issuances, aside from securities backed by mortgages, in 1986 was about:
    a) $1 billion.
    b) $3 billion.
    c) $5 billion.
    d) $10 billion.
    e) $100 billion.

23. Ivanovitch mentions which of these considerations as contributing to globalization of money and capital markets in the future:
    I.   The increased pool of investment outlets due to privatization and debt-equity conversions in the third world.
    II. International operations by brokerage houses.
    III. The increased demand for financial assets due to the growth of mutual funds, pension funds, and other savings media worldwide.
    IV. Round-the-clock trading.
    V.   Increases in the volume of international security analysis.
    a) I and V.
    b) II and III.
    c) III, IV and V.
    d) V.
    e) All of the above.

24. A concern Volcker has about innovative securities is that:
    a) He does not fully understand them, and worries that managers of financial institutions may not as well.
    b) They may promote risk-taking.
    c) They have not yet included securitized bank loans to sovereign nations.
    d) They may distract financial institutions from their traditional lending activities.
    e) Because of the difficulty in analyzing them, it is hard to incorporate consideration of them in assessments of the capital adequacy of financial institutions.

25. In net, Volcker feels that it is fortunate that bank loans to foreign nations have not been securitized because:
    a) They would be acquired by investors who would not understand the risks.
    b) The high discounts on these securities compared to the face value of the loans would show how severe the foreign debt situation is.
    c) Resolution of the problems associated with these debts is better managed within the banking system.
    d) No one would buy the securities.
    e) The coming defaults would merely create financial distress in another sector of the financial system.

Self-Evaluation Examination Answers

See Driscoll

1. d All these factors are mentioned by Driscoll.

See Wruble

2. b Innovations B, securitization of mortgages.
   d Adjustable-rate mortgages, are mentioned by Wruble in his example of how savings and loans have benefitted from innovation.

See Grant

3. b Grant says that the junk bond market is worth approximately $100 billion, selection B, not as big as some have suggested.
4. c Grant says the credit cycle begins with skepticism.
   a Grant says the credit cycle ends with manic optimism.

See Pike

5. e Pike makes a distinction between junk and high-yield bonds according to how they came to have high yields.
6. a Pike notes that while high-yield bonds have had higher defaults than other grades of bonds, these defaults have not been enough to offset initially higher yields, so returns have been high. And volatility of returns have been in line with those of other fixed-income securities.
7. c Pike says the time to sell high-yield bonds is when everyone loves them, but he believes we are not there yet.

See Asay

8. e Asay notes that, ideally, synthetic securities may make cash flows more predictable, but at a minimum they can concentrate the uncertainty about cash flows.
9. e These two strips disentangle coupon rates and prepayment risk, and allow them to be recombined into a wider range of securities forms.
10. b To produce a discount security, the amount of coupon must be reduced relative to the amount of principal. Only B does this.

See Youngblood

11. c
12. a With higher interest rates come lower prepayments, and thus the difference on the what is earned on the mortgages and what is paid on the short tranches persists for a longer period. Moreover, the income earned on undistributed funds increases.

See Miller

13. a Miller notes that gold-backed railroad bonds existed prior to the 1930s.
14. a Miller also mentions D, the availability of long-dated options as a need served by asset-backed securities, but says that A, expanding the opportunity to control the risk-return profile, is more important.
15. c All of these may be potential problems, but Miller specifically mentions the options component valuation difficulty.

See Forrester

16. d Forrester does note that the long-wave properties of the model resemble the Kondratieff cycle.
17. c Economic decline.

See Nelson

18. c
19. c

See Dub

20. e See his Table 8.
21. b Dub mentions the other answers as attractions, and says that lack of familiarity and understanding actually is responsible for the high yields on these securities.
22. d

See Ivanovitch

23. a

See Volcker

24. a
25. c